# Children's Reading Problems

teaching practices which obviously work ought as well to help us when we try to produce psychological explanations of what has gone wrong in the first place. This certainly happened in our own work.

That work has been influenced and helped over the years by a large number of people. The community of people who do research on children's reading problems is as friendly as it is widely scattered. We should like to thank several of them for their advice, for telling us what to read and for disagreeing with us every now and then: Rod Barron and J.P. Das in Canada: Uta Frith, Maggie Snowling and Bill Yule in London: Charles Hulme in York: Philip Seymour in Dundee: Paul Bertelson, Jesus Alegria and Jose Morais in Brussels: Chris Pratt, Alison Garton, Bill Tunmer and Philip Dermody in Australia: Frank Vellutino in America. In Oxford we were inspired and indeed taught by three research students (all long since ex-research students), Charles Hulme, Yuko Kimura and Sue Robertson. Their excellent doctoral theses played an important part in this book. In Oxford too we were helped by many people working clinically with children who have reading problems, and most notably by Jenny Dennis and by Janet Lindsay at the Park Hospital.

Six people read our manuscript at different stages. Sue Somerville struggled with and generously and cleverly helped us to shape the first, rough draft. Terezinha Carraher read the next version and asked the pertinent question, 'But what are backward readers actually like?' That helped us a great deal, and so did the comments of Philip Carpenter – our noble publisher. Bridget Bryant read the last but one and also the last draft and gave us much valuable advice. Among many other comments she pointed out that we had managed to say everything twice – an occupational hazard among university lecturers. Betty Root and Diana Bentley of the highly successful Reading Centre at Reading University also made some pertinent comments on our final draft. So did Uta Frith whose encouragement helped us as much as her work and ideas have always done.

We thank them, and we dedicate our book to the children

who suffer from the problems which we want to help to solve. They face their undeserved difficulties with a wry, good humour. Their eventual successes led us to write this book.

Peter Bryant
Lynette Bradley

# 1

# What is the problem?

Of all the things that children have to learn when they get to school reading and writing are the most basic, the most central and the most essential. Practically everything else that they do there will be permeated by these two skills. Hardly a lesson can be understood, hardly a project finished unless the children can read the books in front of them and write about what they have done. They must read and write or their time at school will be largely wasted.

It is hard to overestimate the sheer pervasiveness of these skills. It is not just that they are needed in every school subject. They may also have a profound effect on the way children think about things and on their acquaintance with their own language. Books set out lines of reasoning with a coherence that must be quite rare in the conversations which young children hear. It is possible that the experience of reading other people's arguments will help children to form their own more logically and effectively. It is quite possible, too, that by dint of reading the child learns things about her own language which she had never realized before. We know that young children have only the haziest notions of linguistic units like words, phrases and sentences. But with the help of spaces and punctuation, words and sentences become quite explicit in print. Here, too, the child may come to understand an important part of her world through the experience of reading.[1]

We do not yet know all of the consequences of learning to read and write, but they must be profound. Examine what anyone knows about the world or what he has learned to do, or even the way he thinks about what happens to him, and you are bound to be impressed by the role the written word has played in all these things. It is hard to think of anything else which could have so broad an effect on children's development as reading.

If reading can have such powerful results so too, but in the opposite direction, does failing to learn to read. It is unfortunate, but such failures do happen and always with the same devastating consequences. We have in our schools a large number of children who find the task of learning to read a fearsome business. Some manage it only with the greatest of difficulty, others not at all. Many of these children have fallen behind on every front. They have usually been slow in learning to speak. Their knowledge of their world is woefully incomplete and their scores in intelligence tests (a very crude index of developmental progress) are distinctly low. It is not at all surprising that children as generally handicapped as this fall behind in reading, compared to others of the same age. Their plight is a serious one and they certainly need and deserve to be helped to learn to read in any way that is possible. But their problem with reading was always to be expected.

At the same time there are other children whose difficulties are a great deal more surprising. They also have appalling problems when they try to learn to read and write, but they are intelligent, quick and alert. They have all the advantages of help and encouragement from their parents. They receive devoted and skilled attention from their teachers. Yet their difficulties persist. Week by week these unfortunate children fall further and further behind their schoolfellows. Faced with written instructions, questions or texts of any sort, their disadvantage is strikingly obvious both to themselves and increasingly to others as well. Usually their predicament is even more serious and certainly much harder to hide whenever they have to write.

We shall call these children – children, that is, whose reading levels fall far below what would have been predicted on other counts such as their intelligence – *backward readers*. Their number is uncomfortably large. In England it varies from area to area, but is high everywhere. From three to five per cent of the children in our schools can be said to have fallen seriously behind in their reading.[2] These large figures do not include those children who on grounds of low intelligence, could reasonably be expected to read badly.

What is one to do about a problem as great as this? It poses two questions. One is how to help children who already have become backward readers over their difficulties. The second is how to prevent these problems arising in the first place. These are practical questions but the answer to them must depend on a proper theoretical understanding of the problem. We need to know what causes reading difficulties.

The question of causes must lie at the heart of any solution to the problem of backwardness in reading. Suppose for a moment that their main trouble is with remembering words and sounds, as many people have in fact suggested.[3] In this case it would be pointless to spend ages teaching these children how to tell alphabetic letters apart visually. One would instead have to think of ways of helping their memory. It is the same with the question of prevention. You can only prevent something happening by removing its source. In the case of reading backwardness this would mean finding out what stops some children from learning to read after they become schoolchildren, and then taking steps to overcome that obstacle before they ever get to school.

All this is uncontroversial. Everyone who has anything to do with the problem wants to find a way of eradicating it. Nearly everyone agrees on the importance of wedding theory to practice. Virtually all the research on the problem has been concerned in one way or another with the question of its causes. Yet for a very long time we have been nowhere near solving it. Now things are changing quickly. We think that a solution is very close – so close, in fact, that we can already discern its shape and many of its details too. Why this has happened, and also why it took so long to happen, is an intriguing story.

## Who are backward readers?

We shall start with a particular child who was without doubt a poor reader.[4] His name is Mark, and he was 13 years old when we saw him a number of years ago. He was a lively and intelligent boy. His score on a standard test showed his intelligence to be above average. Yet he had always had great difficulties with reading and even worse problems with spelling. He read no better than the typical child of 7¼ years and his spelling was equivalent to that of a child of 6¼.

We set about trying to find out more about him, and discovered an intriguing mixture of capacity and incapacity. We shall deal first with the things he was bad at. Two difficulties, apart from his obvious reading and spelling problems, stood out. One was that he often found it hard to remember and produce the right word at the right time. This became obvious when we talked to him. He was fluent enough, but when we questioned him on specific topics he was immediately in difficulty. Though he was adept at filling in and covering up the gaps in his sentences with 'um' and 'you know' and circumlocutions, those gaps were definitely there. He told us that, though never at a loss for words, he often could not think of the right one. His mother said that it had always been so, and that when Mark was young he had amused her by making up his own names for things on the spot. She had called this 'Mark's private language'.

He could not tell us what month it was at the time we saw him, even after he had looked at his watch and found that it was the third month of the year. He could not even tell us the name of the month of his birthday, although he knew it to be the seventh month of the year. He still did not know the names of the letters of the alphabet. His teacher had told us that he often would not answer the questions even when she was sure that he knew the right answer. When we asked him about this he agreed that he usually did know the right answer, but simply could not manage to think of the right words to express it.

Mark's second problem seemed to be with sounds. Words consist of segments of sound: for example, the word 'cat' can be broken up into the three sounds: C – A – T. The alphabet works through these segments of sound. By and large the spoken word's sounds are represented by the written word's letters. Mark had only a dim idea of the way in which words can be broken up into their constituent sounds. His spelling certainly suggested this. He wrote 'thunder' as 'fude' an error which betrays a thoroughly weak grasp of the sounds in that word. We looked at his awareness of constituent sounds in words in another task which had nothing directly to do with reading: we asked him to work out whether words rhymed or, in other words, had sounds in common. He was very bad at this: he could not, for example, work out which of the four words, 'wig', 'fig', 'pin', 'dig', did not rhyme with the rest. Yet this is a task which comes quite easily to a typically intelligent child of only five or six years.

There were things that Mark did well. When we showed him words such as 'high', 'laugh', 'canary' and 'saucer' for a brief time – words which he simply could not read – he could none the less write them out from memory. He obviously remembered very clearly what those words had looked like.

It is easy to see how Mark's weaknesses could have led to his problems with reading (though at this stage we are only speculating). If you cannot think of the right word at the right time you will have difficulty when trying to attach spoken words to written words. There is also a plausible connection to be made between his insensitivity to sounds and his problems with reading. Learning to use the alphabet must depend on knowing how to break up words into their constituent sounds.

Mark's story does not end there. We were able to find ways of helping him tackle his problems, and we shall return to these in chapters 7 and 8. For the moment, we shall simply make the point that he was in many ways a typical example of a poor reader but that he was also a distinct individual with his own particular pattern of strengths and weaknesses.

What did he have in common with other backward readers? There certainly were things about him that are not to be found in many other backward readers. Few have such pronounced difficulty with producing words, although many, but not all, have the same problem about isolating sounds in words.

## Are backward readers unusual? – the question of continuity

Of all the questions to be asked about backward readers this one has the most immediate practical impact. If backward readers really do learn to read in an unusual and idiosyncratic way, then almost certainly we shall have to teach them in an unusual way too. Methods of teaching which work well with other children may be quite wrong for them.

But, one might very well object, we already know that backward readers are unusual. They read unusually poorly. That is right, of course, but by 'unusual' we mean more than this. A well-known conversation between Scott Fitzgerald and Hemingway about wealth captures the distinction. To Fitzgerald's remark that the rich are different from us, Hemingway's riposte was: 'Yes, they have more money than us'. We have exactly the same two possibilities to consider when we come to the difficulties which afflict backward readers.

The first possibility is that the difficulties which backward readers suffer are exactly the same in kind as those encountered by any other child. The only difference is that those of the backward reader are considerably greater. It is Hemingway's alternative: no difference in kind but a large difference in amount.

The second possibility – Scott Fitzgerald's – is that backward readers do not just have more difficulties: they have an altogether different kind of difficulty. The forces which stand in their way are peculiar to them, and have nothing to do with the forces which decide how well and how quickly other children learn to read. If this were true, one would certainly have to look to one's teaching methods. Different difficulties usually require different remedies.

## A continuum – the Hemingway alternative

Let us return to Mark and begin with his apparent insensitivity to the way in which words can be divided up into units of sound. If the Hemingway alternative is right Mark's difficulties with sounds are difficulties which every child has. He just has more of them.

But one can push this further. Mark, we are claiming, reads less well than average because, for some reason, he is less skilled than others at dividing words up into their constituent sounds. But suppose that this is a hurdle for every child – a hurdle which some children are better at crossing than others are. Then their success at getting over the hurdle and understanding the nature of sounds in words might have a powerful effect on their progress in reading. Those who are particularly slow at it like Mark will end up reading well below expectations, whereas those who cross the hurdle unusually quickly will do very much better than expected when they begin to learn to read. In other words there may be what we call *a continuum* going from children who are very poor at analysing sounds and read poorly through to children whose skill with sounds is roughly average and read as well as expected, and on to children who are particularly good with sounds and consequently much better at reading than one would normally expect.

There are lots of reasons for wanting to know if such a continuum does exist, but the most pressing are practical. If it does and the same forces affect good and backward readers alike, what is good for one child should be good for all children. One still has to find the right teaching method, but one does not have to worry too much about whom it would suit. It should suit everyone. This is important, because in that case the main stumbling block for prevention would be removed.

One would no longer have to bother about identifying a special group of children needing special attention. You would simply have to find out the best way to help children – all children – to prepare themselves for reading. That is a great deal easier and it would also help more people.

## Unusual and idiosyncratic reading – the Scott Fitzgerald alternative

Special conditions, in contrast, demand special treatment. Backward readers might be held back by forces which play no part at all in determining the progress of the other 95 per cent or so of our schoolchildren. In that case there ought to be special forms of teaching which would help the backward readers over their idiosyncratic hurdles, but which would not be the slightest use to other children.

Such idiosyncrasies might well exist. There is no reason why there has to be a continuum. Mark's difficulties could be a case in point. Take as an example one of his two symptoms – his slowness to find the right word at the right time. Let us assume that we are right in our guess that this, too, held his reading back. The Scott Fitzgerald view would be that the skill of finding the right word is only relevant to Mark and to a few other backward readers like him. It might play little or no part in determining how well or poorly most other children read. They all have the skill to a reasonable degree: it comes to them as naturally as breathing. They have to breathe to read, but how well they breathe does not make them good or average readers. In just the same way they have to remember and to produce the right words in order to read, but how well they do so may have no effect on how well the vast majority of them learn to read. If this alternative were right, Mark would be helped a great deal by being taught how to come up with the appropriate word quickly. But exactly the same teaching would have no effect at all on other children's reading.[5]

Now that we have made the distinction between these two points of view we should mention some things which both have in common or which at any rate do not distinguish the two. Neither questions the seriousness of these children's plight or their need for help. It is sometimes thought that those who dislike the notion of a separate group also belittle the problems which afflict the poor reader. That is not true. They are as keen as anyone else to help. The disagreement is about how to study these children and how to help them.

Then there is the use of the term 'dyslexia'. The term fits the idea of a separate and distinct group better than it does a continuum. We have the impression that the people who hold to the former are readier than most to call poor readers 'dyslexics', but there is no clear dividing line. There are people who accept the idea that poor readers are just one extreme end of a continuum and still call them 'dyslexics'.[6] The word is used so generally nowadays that it does not commit anyone to a point of view. We thought it best to talk about 'backward readers', but that was not a particularly significant decision.

Finally everyone concerned with these children agrees that we have to find out more about the underlying reasons for their difficulties. How to do that properly is the subject of the next chapter.

### Notes

1 There is an interesting, though speculative, account of the possible effects of learning to read and write on children's understanding of language in the book by Gunther Kress, *Learning to write* (1982).
2 The best information on the numbers of these children is to be found in the papers by Rutter and Yule (1975), by Yule and his colleagues (1974), and by Rodgers (1983).
3 The 1983 paper by Jorm makes the claim about a difficulty in memory in a comprehensive and enthusiastic way.
4 You will find a fuller account of Mark's difficulties and progress in the paper by Bradley, Hulme and Bryant (1979).
5 One way of looking at the question of continuity is through large-scale epidemiological studies. The well-known Isle of Wight study, which is described in the paper by Yule et al. (1974) and in the following review by Rutter and Yule (1975) did suggest the existence of a special group of children whose reading had fallen behind. However this may have been a function of the reading

test that they used, which was too easy, and there are now other and contradictory results (see the paper by Rodgers).

6 Andy Ellis makes this point convincingly in his recent book, *Reading, Writing and Dyslexia* (1984).

# 2

# Getting the evidence right

When we described the case of Mark we could only speculate about the reasons for his slowness in reading. Now we must consider how to establish whether this sort of speculation is right or not. How does one find convincing evidence about the reasons for children's reading difficulties?

In the end everything in our book turns on this question. We have to get the evidence right, and one of our main points will be that, on the whole, people have not got it right in the past. People have often used quite inadequate evidence to support their ideas about the causes of reading problems, and it has often taken a great deal of time for the rest of us to realize how misleading these ideas are.

That is why we are taking the unusual and rather daunting step of writing a whole chapter about how to get the evidence right so early in the book. Some kinds of evidence are convincing, and some are downright misleading. We want to make the distinction between the two as clear as possible from the start.

## The idea of the deficit

We shall begin with an assumption which pervades every discussion of the plight of the backward reader. There have been many different ideas about the underlying causes of reading difficulties, but all of them take the same general form. They all appeal to the notion of the deficit or defect.

Let us start with the example of one of the first causal theories about backward readers. 'The defect in these children is then a strictly specialised one, viz. a difficulty in acquiring and storing up in the brain the visual memories of words and letters.' Here is as firm a claim about the causes of the problem as one could wish for, and it was made very early on, at the turn of the century, by Hinshelwood, a Scottish eye surgeon. He was one of the first people to show an interest in the problems of intelligent children who unexpectedly fail to learn to read. No doubt his idea that it can all be traced back to vision was heavily influenced by his own professional preoccupations. It is, as we shall see, certainly wrong.

The point that we are making here is that Hinshelwood was looking for a defect. Something was wrong – there was some basic flaw – with the children's nervous system. Some crucial capacity, a visual one in this case, was said to be missing. This notion has dominated research on children's reading problems ever since. Research workers do not agree on what it is that is missing in the backward readers' psychological repertoire, but they do share the assumption that some deficit or other must be responsible for backwardness in reading.

It is easy to see what led to this assumption and why it has held such sway over the years. Its starting point is always the large number of skills that are involved in learning to read. Reading makes many very different demands on the child and so depends on a number of different skills. He must, for example, be able to distinguish and to remember the visual appearance of different letters and words; he has to work out how the alphabetic letters symbolize different sounds and how these sounds can be put together to make words; he must be able to learn a host of rules about spelling; and he will also soon have to use his knowledge of his language to make intelligent guesses about the meaning of difficult words in prose passages. This is by no means the end of what soon becomes a very long list, but we have said enough for the moment to make the point that learning to read even the simplest of sentences is bound to involve several very different skills. Perception, memory, breaking words up into their constituent sounds, linking spoken with written patterns, learning rules (and coming to terms with the many exceptions to these rules), making linguistic inferences – these are skills which seem to have little to do with each other but which must come together when children begin to read.

They are all needed then, and that is what makes the idea of a deficit so appealing. After all, we have to be able to explain not only why these children cannot read well, but also why at the same time they are manifestly intelligent and capable and can cope with things which involve no reading perfectly well. The idea of deficits copes with this problem. It is easy to imagine a child whose repertoire of human skills is, with one small exception, virtually normal managing successfully for most of the time.

The idea is equally congenial to those who hold the notion of a continuum and to those who do not. The deficit may be in a skill which plays an important part in deciding all children's relative success in reading (the continuum) or it may not. Either way it would hold back the backward reader. But having stated the idea, one must decide how to show that it is right. That is where matters become complicated.


## Showing a difference

If some particular deficit were responsible for children's reading difficulties, then backward readers should in one specific way at least be quite different from other children. Let us for the sake of argument take one completely hypothetical possibility. Suppose that it were all a matter of memory, and that backward readers had an appalling memory for words, that stopped them learning which words went with which sets of symbols. (In fact, several people, such as Anthony Jorm in his 1979 and 1983 papers and D.J. Bakker have suggested variants of just this theory.) In that case it should be possible to take a group of backward readers, test their memory in some task which does not involve reading, look at the way other children manage this same task and show that the backward readers are really very much worse at it than children who have no reading problems.

Most research on children's reading problems has taken exactly this form. People have taken groups of backward readers and compared them to other children in the hope of finding some specific difference between the two groups which could then be used to explain the original reading problem. It seems a perfectly reasonable thing to do. If backward readers do suffer from a specific deficit, it ought to be possible to demonstrate that deficit in a precise and controlled way.

However there is a snag. Reading problems not only have causes: they have effects too. Most children from the age of six onwards are bombarded with written information in the form of books, newspapers and even advertisements, about their world. Backward readers are cut off from most of this. There may well be emotional consequences too. As time goes on, children who fall behind in reading are bound to become more and more aware of their own failure. Surely all this could have the most drastic consequences. Thus whenever we come across some difference between children with reading difficulties and children who read without any great problem, there is one question that we must ask: *Does this difference tell us about the causes of reading difficulties or is it one of its consequences?*

Most studies of the problems of backward readers come nowhere near making this essential distinction. The subject is plagued by ambiguity – the ambiguity of not being able to say what leads to what. Let us take a concrete example. One of the most popular and most influential ideas about backward readers in recent years has been a rather general one about their language. There is a well-known theory, developed by Frank Vellutino, that the root of the problem is a 'verbal deficit'. The general idea is plausible enough. Reading and writing are linguistic tasks. What could be more natural than the possibility that the backward reader's problems are due to a particular thing wrong with the way he learned to speak or to understand speech?

One piece of evidence for the idea has always been the children's performance in different parts of intelligence tests.

These tests are often divided into a 'verbal' part in which the questions put to the children and the answers that they give have to be couched in words (a vocabulary test: 'What does "donkey" mean?', 'bicycle'?, 'thief'?, or a test of similarities: 'How are an apple and an orange alike?', are typical examples), and a non-verbal part in which the children usually have to rearrange spatial, jig-saw like material without having to say anything at all.

When backward readers are put through such tests and compared to children of the same age and overall ability, the backward readers as a group produce worse scores than the other children in the verbal tests. The difference is hard and fast, and has been reproduced in many studies and in several different countries. We can be absolutely sure that on the whole backward readers do fall behind in verbal tests and therefore do have a relatively low 'verbal intelligence', whatever that means.

It was a short step from this discovery to the claim that the verbal problem causes the children's difficulties with reading. The claim is now widely accepted and the result that we have described has even been used as one of the bases for the hypothesis that there is something the matter with the left half of the backward readers' brain – the part of the brain which usually is most responsible for language.

But to produce a theory of this sort is to take another step. It is one thing to say that backward readers do worse in verbal than in non-verbal tests, and quite a different thing to claim that this is a cause of their reading difficulties. The first statement cannot be disputed: the second definitely can. It ought to be disputed because there is a clear alternative. These verbal difficulties could easily be the result of the child's failure to learn to read. After all, a child who learns to read successfully must as a result have linguistic experiences which the backward reader is denied. That difference in experiences could lead to different results in verbal intelligence tests.

Is there a way round the difficulty? It seems to us that there are two ways. One is to pursue the 'showing a difference' kind of study, but in a more radical form. The other is to turn to quite different methods.

The radical version of the kind of study that we have just been describing is not always viable, but when it works it is an extremely powerful technique. It will crop up quite a lot in other parts of this book. We shall describe it only briefly here. One takes, for example, a group of ten-year-old backward readers who are, say, two years behind in reading and so read at the level of a typical eight year old. One compares them to a group of eight-year-old children who, being typical children, also read at the eight-year-old level. Both groups then have reached the same level of reading. This means that any evidence for some deficit or other in the group of backward readers cannot be the result of a difference in reading level, for the simple reason that there is no difference.

If you ever find backward readers worse at some task than children at the same reading level as them, then you can be sure that you have discovered something significant. But such studies are very difficult to do: the backward readers may hide a genuine deficit because they are older and more cunning and have found other ways of coping with the test. Nevertheless there is a handful of studies of this sort.

There is a useful, though technical, term for the method which is '*the reading-age match*'. This simply means that the two groups are at the same level of reading. In contrast, the method which we are criticizing for being thoroughly ambiguous is called '*the mental-age match*', because it compares backward readers with other children of the same age and intelligence (and thus of the same mental age).

## Predicting failure and success

A cause precedes its effect: if *A* causes *B*, *A* must come before *B*. So if *A* genuinely does lead to reading problems it ought to be possible to detect its existence some time before children begin to learn to read and before the backward readers begin to fail to read. The kind of study which takes advantage of this is called 'longitudinal'. It deals with the same children over a period of time. The most interesting period to choose in longitudinal studies of learning to read goes from the time before children go to school and begin to learn to read through to several years after they have arrived at school. Longitudinal studies measure children's ability to do something before they are taught to read and show us whether there is any relationship between this and their later success or failure in reading.

We can look at one example of the way the longitudinal method can produce good evidence by going back to the idea of the 'verbal deficit'. That deficit, if the hypothesis is correct, should be there before the difficulties begin and therefore before the child starts to learn to read. So, we have good reason to ask whether the verbal – non-verbal differences can be found before these children start to learn to read.

The evidence is none too clear but what we do have suggests that the verbal – non-verbal differences *follow* the experience of learning or failing to learn to read – a pattern which goes against the idea that verbal deficits cause reading problems. Dorothy Bishop and George Butterworth saw a large number of four-and-a-half-year-old children in the Midlands and gave them an intelligence test called the WPPSI (Wechsler Pre-school and Primary Scale of Intelligence) which measures verbal and non-verbal intelligence separately. Then they saw them again four years later, and measured the children's reading skills and also once again their intelligence (this time using the WISC (Wechsler Intelligence Scale for Children) which is devised by the same people as was the earlier test and is similar to it). The second time round, when the children were eight, Bishop and Butterworth found that the verbal tests were more closely related to reading than were the non-verbal ones and also that the backward readers were worse at the verbal than at the other tests. But when these two investigators looked back at the four-year-olds' scores they found a very different picture. Both parts of the test were equally related to the children's eventual success in reading, and the children who were to become backward readers were not at the time particularly weak in the verbal tests. Their eventual 'verbal deficit' came after they began to learn to read, not before. It looks very much as though it was the consequence and not the cause of the reading problem.

This interesting piece of work demonstrates the value of longitudinal studies. We do, however, have to sound one note of caution about the method. A discovery that one thing precedes and is related to another is not on its own enough to establish a cause beyond any doubt. We have to consider the problem of what is often called the *'tertium quid'*. Suppose that you find some measure that predicts whether a child is to become a backward reader before he begins to read. This does not necessarily mean that what you are measuring, $A$, causes reading difficulties, $B$. The alternative is that both things – the existence of $A$ in a child and his reading problems, $B$ – are determined by some other unknown third factor, $C$. Neither $A$ nor $B$ in this case would be the cause of the other. They are simply related through $C$, the third factor, about which nothing is known. One should not ignore this awkward possibility.

## Intervention

There is a way round the difficulty of the unknown third factor. The solution lies in the training study. We shall have much to say about training later on, so for the moment we shall stick to the logic of such studies. If some skill such as memory does determine how well children read, then improving their memory should also have the consequence of making their reading better as well. For example, train some children who may or may not be backward readers in what interests you and make sure that you have a control group of children who are given the same amount of attention and the same kind of experiences except for the experience which you think crucial to reading. Then, later, measure their reading skills, and if your hypothesis is right the first group of children, trained in what interests you, should as a consequence be reading more successfully than the others. The logic is impeccable and the method has the added advantage, when successful, of producing immediate practical recommendations about successful ways of teaching children.

We have one example of such a study. Some time ago Jenny Hewison and Jack Tizard looked at the amount of time that parents spent listening to their children reading. They found that the more the parents did this, the better on the whole their children were at reading. This raised the possibility that the parents' willingness to listen has a direct and beneficial effect on their children's reading. The research workers then turned to intervention to see if this were true. They actively encouraged parents of one group of children, the 'experimental' group, to listen to them reading regularly. The study also included a 'control' group of children who were given extra tuition for reading in their classroom over the same period. At the end of the study the first group of children had made more progress in reading than the other children.

This is good evidence that experiences at home can affect reading. One can cavil about certain parts of the study. It would have been better if the control group had had as much extra contact over books with their parents as the experimental group had. Otherwise one cannot be sure that it is actually the experience of reading to the parent which brought on the children in the experimental group. None the less something about the contact between children and their parents obviously did have a powerful effect in this study, and that is good evidence that there are experiences at home which influence the way children learn to read. This does not mean, of course, that reading difficulties can be traced back to the home. But it does suggest that in general the home plays a role in children's reading. We shall return to this idea later on. For the moment our point is that intervention studies are a powerful tool in the search for causes.

However, they too have a weakness, which is that they run the risk of being artificial. We often cannot tell whether the experiences which children are given in intervention studies have much relationship to what goes on in real life outside the laboratory. There is a solution to this problem as we shall see in the next section.

## The solution

Our solution is to combine different methods. Each has its own strengths and weaknesses, but fortunately these are complementary. The strengths of one method make up for the weakness of another. We start with a (hypothetical) study of backward readers. Using the correct reading-age match, it shows some genuine difference between these and other children. Backward readers are weak in some particular skill. Now we want to know whether this skill plays an important part in determining other children's relative success in reading, and so we do a large-scale study, preferably a longitudinal one, to see how well this skill predicts their progress in learning to read. Let us assume that the relationship between these two things – the skill and progress in reading – is strong. We know that there is an association between the two (the method's strength), but we cannot be sure that the association is a causal one (the method's weakness).

So we turn to another method, intervention. We teach the skill to see if doing so affects reading. If it does and if the controls are right, we know that the increase in the skill has caused an improvement in reading (this method's strength) but we cannot be certain that this causal relationship really does exist outside our laboratory and in the real world (this method's weakness).

Now we can see that the strengths of each method make up for the weaknesses of the other. The longitudinal study shows that there is a relationship in real life, and the training study establishes that that relationship is genuinely causal. Neither method on its own can tell the whole story, but put together they add up to a formidable tool. We shall see exactly how formidable it can be in the next two chapters.

# 3

# Is there a deficit?

There is a characteristic form to books on children's reading problems. It stems from the one thing that they have in common – the assumption that a deficit or a set of deficits is responsible for the problems. Different chapters, different deficits, is the pattern of these books and their usual aim is to identify the most significant deficit of all. 'Hunt the deficit' is the dominant theme.

This will be our 'Hunt the deficit' chapter. We ourselves have doubts about the notion, and in chapter 5 we shall try to show that other obstacles besides the deficit face backward readers. However in this and in the next chapter we shall stick closely to the idea of the deficit and shall try at the same time to answer two questions. One is simply whether there is any good evidence for the idea. The other is about the issue of continuity and discontinuity. We need to know if the skills in which backward readers are notably weak do play a significant part in the relative success and failure of other children's reading.

## Are backward readers afflicted by specific deficits?

Many deficits have been suggested, and over the years the focus of these suggestions has changed. Originally they concentrated on the possibility that backward readers do not see or hear things properly. Nowadays we hear much more about problems with language and with rule learning. We have moved from 'perceptual' to 'verbal' or 'conceptual' deficits. The reason for this shift is easy to understand. Originally everyone hoped for some peripheral peculiarity, easy to detect and as easy to put right. They thought that there must be some oddity in the way in which these children take in patterns visually or hear the words which have to be linked to these patterns. But as these hopes were dashed thoughts turned to the possibility of a less tangible and a less accessible kind of deficit. People began to ask whether backward readers are slow to learn rules in general and linguistic rules in particular.

Let us begin, as the subject began, with hypotheses about deficits in visual perception. The reasons for the initial interest in vision have as much to do with educational history as with anything else. It was only after the introduction of universal education in this country that it gradually became clear that there were some intelligent children who remained virtually illiterate even though they were given all the benefits of school education. But what was to be done with these puzzling children? There were no psychologists at the time, and nothing much in the way of remedial education. Doctors seemed the only possible source of help and, since reading and writing both involve visual patterns, the most appropriate doctors were deemed to be those who dealt with the visual system.

The first idea was that these children might not be seeing things properly. The metaphor of blindness stalks the first accounts of the problem by Hinshelwood and Morgan. 'Word blindness' and 'mind blindness' were their terms respectively, and this was to be expected given that their main interest was in the workings of the visual system. But these early explanations made little headway. If you want to demonstrate something amiss with the way backward readers see things, then you have to show that this idiosyncrasy exists quite independently of reading. This Hinshelwood and Morgan failed to do and, as we shall see, it is something that no one else has managed to do since.

## Directional deficits

Soon, however, someone did produce the idea of a very specific visual difficulty, which could in principle hold back reading and yet have virtually no damaging effect on any other aspect of the child's behaviour. This was Samuel Orton, an American neurologist – also an expert on vision. He was particularly struck by what are known as mirror image confusions. He claimed that backward readers tend to be muddled about the direction of letters and words, hence to confuse, for example, 'p' with 'q', 'd' with 'b' and, in the case of words, 'saw' with 'was'. 'Dyslexia rules, K.O.?', one of the most delightful of graffiti (even if it is apocryphal), neatly illustrates Orton's observation and demonstrates the wide credence still given to it.

He gave the name of 'strephosymbolia' – the twisting of symbols – to this confusion, and he meant it literally because he thought that backward readers see patterns now in the corrections direction, now in the reversed and twisted way. Orton also had an explanation for this 'twisting' which he couched in neurophysiological terms, which concerned the left and right halves of the brain. The brain consists of a right and a left hemisphere which are symmetrical anatomically and thus are mirror images of each other. Orton thought that there must be some connection between this mirror image arrangement of the brain's hemispheres and the confusion which he saw backward readers making between mirror image pairs of letters such as 'b' and 'd'. He argued that when a backward reader looks at a letter the message about it in one hemisphere is the mirror image of the message about the same letter in the other hemisphere. The child thus has two images, one the mirror image of the other, and this is bound to confuse him when he has to distinguish actual mirror images like 'p' and 'q'.

Why do these pairs not confuse normal readers? Orton's answer is that it is all a matter of the maturity of the brain. Normally as children grow older the left and right halves of the brain perform different functions, and this, he claimed, allows children a way of distinguishing the two hemispheres and thus of overcoming mirror image confusions. He also argued that this development of the brain is slower in children who become backward readers, and that is why they are prey to the confusions which struck him so forcibly.

His theory held considerable sway and still has something of an influence, at any rate on graffiti writers, but it does not work. For one thing it is now clear that the kind of mistake which Orton thought to be so important accounts for a very small proportion of the reading errors committed by young children as a whole. The figure is always below 15 per cent. Another problem is the logic of the theory itself. It is dubious because the theory seems to depend on the existence of a little person in the brain looking confusedly at the images in either hemisphere. That would be the only possible reason for confusing mirror image messages in the two hemispheres.[2]

But this rather sophisticated objection need not occupy us long because there is another, and much more compelling, reason for abandoning Orton's deficit. It is that the original observation on which Orton based his theory is wrong. Children with reading problems are no more prone to mirror image reversals when they read letters, words and sentences than other children are, and the same goes for writing. Direct comparisons even between poor and normal readers of the same age (and mental age) show no difference in the proportion of 'reversal' errors that the two groups of children make. The fact is that all children, and not just the child who falls behind in reading, make such mistakes. They are not the reason why he falls behind in his reading.

But though Orton's theory was in many ways a false start, it did have one good and lasting effect. It led him to the idea of multisensory methods as a way of teaching backward readers. The main aim of this form of teaching is to involve as many senses as possible when showing the child how to recognize and to write words. Movement, touch, hearing and vision are all as far as possible actively and simultaneously involved. Orton developed this method, together with his colleague,

Anna Gillingham, because he thought it would speed up the development of the backward reader's nervous system. His rationale for the method may have been quite wrong, but the method itself has produced some impressive results. We shall be looking at these in chapter 7.

## General visual deficits

If the direction of letters and words is not a serious problem for backward readers is there any other visual weakness which might be holding them back? The only alternative to have been considered at all seriously is that they have some general difficulty with distinguishing and remembering visual patterns. This type of problem would certainly have serious repercussions as obviously any child who tends to confuse visual patterns will find it hard to remember which alphabetic letter is which. But there could be another even more serious consequence of a visual problem like this.

It is extremely improbable that we read words letter by letter, one after the other. We may have to do this occasionally when we meet a completely new word, but most of the time we are almost certainly dealing in groups of letters which might be highly familiar such as '-ing', or might correspond to whole words. It seems quite probable that this might be something that children grasp very early on. After all, they are bombarded with the sight of words and written patterns like 'STOP', 'School', 'EXIT' and 'BBC', and there seems nothing to stop them learning these words as wholes, rather than laboriously converting each letter into a sound.

Presumably reading in groups of letters has the advantage of speed and economy, but there is another powerful reason why it might help us to cope with written English. Some words can be read simply by putting together the sounds associated with their individual letters. 'Cat' is one. When the sounds which typically go with these three letters are combined, they add up to a sound very like the word 'cat'. But words like this are comparatively rare in written English. Let us take another common word, 'light'. It is quite hard to arrive at the right answer here simply by adding up the sounds unless, perhaps, one is used to pronouncing the word in an exaggerated Scottish accent. At the letter-by-letter level written English is a very irregular system indeed. Letters such as 'i', 'g', 'h' and 't' signify different sounds in different words. But longer sequences such as '-ight' are a great deal more consistent. To know that a particular sound goes with a sequence like this is to have learned quite a reliable rule, even if it is just a rule of thumb. It is certainly a great deal more reliable than anything one learns about the sounds typically associated with letters such as 'i' or 'g'. Chunks of one sort and another could very well play a crucial role in learning to read and, one should also note, to spell.

What has this to do with vision or with the question of visual deficits? The answer is that one possible way of recognizing a chunk when you see it is by its overall shape. This is a very familiar idea, and it lay behind the development of the 'whole word' teaching method, which was founded on the conviction that the most efficient unit in reading is the word, that words can be recognized by their overall shapes, that young children are certainly very good at recognizing shapes, and that the sooner young children are taught to take advantage of this natural ability when reading the better.

In fact it is not at all clear from the evidence we have that shape is a crucial cue in learning. The question is still a controversial one,[3] but this need not bother us because the answer to the question whether backward readers suffer from an overall visual deficit which prevents them from distinguishing and remembering words as patterns, is an unambiguous 'No'. All the evidence which does suggest that backward readers might be particularly bad at perceiving or remembering shapes comes from experiments with the wrong design. They use the mental-age match. All involve comparisons between backward and normal readers of the same age and with different reading abilities, which means that any difference between the two groups is not to be trusted because it might equally be the cause or the result of the problem.

Let us take just one example, an experiment by Jack Lyle and Judith Goyen in Australia. They showed children one shape at a time for a very brief period, and asked them to choose the same shape from a group of five alternative shapes. Backward readers of 6 and 7 years fared rather worse in this task than did other children of the same age who had no reading difficulties. Here, the experimenters concluded, was evidence for a visual deficit. But we can see straightaway how dubious a result like this is. The visual problem, if there is one, could easily be the product of these children's lack of success in reading.

One's doubts grow apace in the face of further evidence which shows that backward readers cope very well with many tasks which should have caused them great difficulty had they been suffering from a visual deficit. We owe much of this evidence to Frank Vellutino, whose book *Dyslexia* contains a sustained and convincing attack on the idea of a visual deficit. Here, in brief, are some of the results of his own research. Backward readers copy Hebrew letters (unfamiliar to them since these were American children trying to learn to read English) as accurately as other children of the same age. They are no worse either at copying English letters or letter sequences or even words, though they were at once in difficulty if they had to say what the words were. They were at no disadvantage at all when they had to remember unfamiliar patterns like Hebrew words. All in all, when the crucial information in these tasks was just visual the backward readers coped well. All of this suggests very strongly that there is no marked visual deficit here.

There is something of an irony here. In these experiments Vellutino made exactly the kind of comparison (the mental-age match) on which we have poured some scorn: his comparisons were between children of the same age and overall intellectual level, the only difference being in their reading level – the traditional design. Yet now we are drawing from these results the firm conclusion that there is no visual deficit. Is this not annoyingly inconsistent if not downright hypocritical of us?

In fact it is not. One has to distinguish *positive* from *negative* results. Positive results involve the discovery of some difference between backward and normal readers, which is then used to support claims for deficits in backward readers. This is precisely what we have been criticizing. To find no difference between the groups is of course to produce a negative result, and as it turns out this is a result which is as conclusive as positive results are inconclusive. For, if backward readers are no worse than others on this measure despite their poor progress in reading, one can be sure that what is being measured has nothing to do with the causes of reading backwardness. And that is exactly what happens in the case of visual deficits.

We leave this section with two conclusions. One is that it is extremely unlikely that any visual deficit is responsible for backwardness in reading. The other, a more general one, is that the traditional type of experiment which uses the mental-age match does have some part to play. It does at least help us to rule out some candidates for deficits.

## Cross-modal deficits

One other candidate for a perceptual deficit – once widely accepted – can be ruled out in just this way. This is the notion of a 'cross-modal' or an 'intermodal' deficit. Cross-modal perception is the technical term for the simple and obvious fact that we make connections between different senses. We know that a shape which we feel with our hands to be round is identical to a shape that we can see to be round. We easily treat the two types of information – one tactual, the other visual – as equivalent. It is the same with many of the things that we see and hear. We know someone by her voice and by her appearance, and we realize that these two kinds of information mean the same thing – her presence. Thus when we deal with children's perceptual skills we have to think not just about how well they see or hear things, but also about the connections that they can make between what they see and what they hear.

That concern is obligatory when we think of reading. After all, reading depends on a connection between written letters and words which we see, and sounds and spoken words which we hear. It follows that a child's reading could conceivably be held back just because she had difficulty with that kind of connection. This was the idea of Herb Birch, a well-known American child psychologist, who introduced the idea of an 'intermodal deficit'. He thought that backward readers were particularly insensitive to the connections between different types of perception, so that when they saw and heard something at the same time they probably would not understand the association between the two kinds of perceptual experience. This difficulty, he argued, would be a major stumbling block to learning how to read.

He tested this idea with a task that became very well known and was often repeated. The child first hears an auditory pattern, and then sees several visual ones. She has to say which of these visual patterns represents the original auditory pattern most closely. What happened was that the experimenter at first tapped out a sort of inverted morse code pattern with a pencil. He tapped three, four or five times and left either long or short intervals between each tap. This was the auditory pattern. An example would be four taps, the first followed by a long interval and the next two by short intervals. Next came the visual patterns, each consisting of a number of dots separated either by a long or a short space. The task was to say which visual pattern was equivalent to the auditory pattern. In the example that we have just used the correct visual pattern could be: ● ● ● ●.

This task was given to 11-year-old children some of whom had fallen behind in reading. It proved particularly difficult for the backward readers. Birch concluded that backward readers were relatively bad at making intermodal connections, and went on to claim that it was this 'intermodal deficit' which held back their reading.

However there are several pressing reasons for doubting the claim. One is that Birch, like most people at that time, relied on the wrong kind of comparison. Once again we meet an experiment in which the two groups were the same age, while one had a lower reading level than the other. Once again we have to note that there is nothing to be said about cause and effect here. He thought that the weakness in connecting vision and hearing led to backward reading, but it could easily have been the other way round.

Birch's use of the crude age match does not by any means exhaust the problems which beset this infuriating study. There was no guarantee even that the difficulty of the backward readers was anything to do with crossing from hearing to vision: in fact there is now a great deal of evidence to suggest that it was not. The trouble is that the children might have found it difficult either to take in the original pattern of taps or to distinguish between the three visual patterns, or to understand that they had to go from left to right with these patterns. Any one of these things could have caused their poor performance. There is even a further explanation which is that they could have had some difficulty in translating temporal intervals (between the taps) into spatial intervals (between the dots) – a problem of connections between space and time and not between sight and hearing. It is quite easy to test all these possibilities by adding other tasks to see how well the children distinguish patterns of taps or connect temporal with spatial patterns.

When eventually Martin Bryden did an experiment which catered for all these possibilities it showed quite unambiguously that backward readers were at no specific disadvantage when faced with tasks which crossed from hearing to vision or vice versa. They just seemed generally poor at coping with dots and taps. They were worse than normal readers on intermodal tasks, it is true, but they were worse as well on the other tasks which involved only hearing or only vision. But even this nebulous positive result means nothing because Bryden's experiment made the traditional kind of comparison which confuses cause and effect. We can at least draw one firm conclusion from its negative results: backward readers do not suffer from an intermodal deficit.[4]

## Linguistic deficits

Our conclusions so far are not particularly controversial, even
if our reasons for reaching them are not all that orthodox. We
have decided that there is no good basis for the idea that a
perceptual deficit is responsible for reading backwardness. So
do most recent commentaries on the subject. Once the idea
used to dominate the subject: now its proponents are few
indeed. It has been abandoned because even the traditional
experiments which are kind – too kind – to the idea of the
deficit have lent it so little support.

From here on, however, our agreement with the current
consensus will end, for we shall be dealing with ideas which
have a very wide following today but which seem to us to be
houses built on sand. These claims are about several kinds of
deficit in language. Their sandy foundations for the most part
are experiments of the traditional kind which confuse cause
with effect.

There are certainly good reasons for suspecting that a
child's linguistic abilities may be closely connected to his
progress in learning to read and write. After all, he is learning
about the written form of language which he began to speak
four years or so before. Nothing could seem more plausible
than the suggestion that some oddity in his knowledge of
spoken language might prevent him learning about the
written version later on. This suggestion becomes even more
compelling when one remembers the fact that the most
reliable information that we have about backward readers is
that their verbal abilities are in some way different from those
of other children. Every epidemiological study and indeed
every large-scale study that includes comprehensive information about their intelligence demonstrates this. There are
individual children who are exceptions to this pattern but the
average scores point towards the possibility of a linguistic
weakness of some sort.

But we have already seen that this evidence proves nothing
on its own. We need a proper test of cause and effect and

above all we need to have some idea of a mechanism. That is exactly the gap which several psychologists have been trying to fill in recent years. There are several quite different types of hypothesis about possible linguistic deficits. We shall deal with them one by one.

## Word production

The most basic perhaps are those hypotheses which deal with word production. This forbidding term conceals the simple idea that there is more to language than just knowing the right words. We have to be able to produce these right words when we speak, and to produce them within a certain time. Reading at any reasonable speed must require much the same standards. Not only do we have to decipher letters or recognize letter sequences, but we must also think of the words which go with these sequences. Any serious hitch would certainly hamper reading and learning to read.

Several psychologists have made a claim for this hitch. One is to be found in the work of Martha Denckla and Rita Rudel in New York. They decided to test what they called 'Rapid Automatized Naming'. To do this they showed each child a series of 'lists' of drawings of very familiar things (colours, well-known objects, numerals and alphabetic letters). All that the child had to do was to name each thing in the lists as quickly as possible. They gave this task to three groups of children, all of normal intelligence: one was a group of backward readers, another consisted of children who had learning problems at school but who were competent at reading, and the third was a group of children with no particular problems – a control group. The children ranged in age from 7 to 12 years.

Two things happened. The backward readers were slower than children of the same age in the other groups, and in all three groups the younger children were slower than the older ones. The authors were plainly more interested in the first of these two results, and used it as an explanation for children's failures in reading. They argued that children have to learn to associate spoken words with the overall shapes of written words – the whole word method – and that the slower they are in producing words for themselves the harder it will be for them to make this sort of link. Hence their slow production of words stops them learning to read.

It is a coherent idea, but quite inadequately tested here. All the comparisons were between backward readers and other children *of the same age and intelligence*, the only difference being in the groups' reading levels. Once again the difference might have been the result of the difference in reading levels rather than its cause. This is not a far-fetched alternative, for after all reading must give children extensive practice in thinking up the right words speedily.

Ironically Denckla and Rudel actually had data which they could have used to make a much better test of their own idea. They had such a wide range of ages that it would have been possible to compare some of the backward readers to other, younger, children with the same reading level. This would have eliminated all possible effects of the children being at different reading levels.

This disappointing start does not rule out every possible linguistic deficit. There are many other possible ways for the child's language system to go wrong. One, which we referred to briefly in chapter 2, is that some children might be particularly weak at remembering words or sounds, and as a direct consequence fail in reading. Again the hypothesis is coherent, but how has it fared?

## Memory for words

The strongest supporter of this hypothesis is the psychologist A.F. Jorm, who works in Australia. In 1979 he published a paper in which he argued persuasively that a connection should be made between the difficulties of the child who is slow to learn to read and those of adults who lose the ability to read as a result of damage to their brain. Jorm was struck by the way in which the problems for both typically revolve around language. Often adults with brain damage have difficulties remembering words which they have just heard, and one of Jorm's main examples was how difficult it also seemed to be for the child with reading difficulties to remember words at all well. He appealed to several studies in which just this claim was made and wrote another paper that sets out these studies in some detail.

But once again we have to use the expression 'once again'. Jorm's influential claim for the importance of memory is based on experiments which compare backward readers with other children whose age is the same but whose reading level is higher. It is perfectly true that if you read out a set of words or a set of numbers to backward readers they often do not remember them as well as do other children of the same age. But the better memory of the children who read well could easily be the result of their reading experiences. When a child reads a sentence he has to keep the first words in mind until he gets to its end. Reading gives children practice in remembering words: it could have a profound effect on their memory.

Perhaps the clearest example and certainly the best known is the work of Bakker in Holland. One of several studies by him will serve as an example. He worked with 13-year-old children of average intelligence levels whom he divided into two groups. The children in one group were much worse at reading than those in the other group. His purpose was to look at their memory for a series of meaningful patterns and a series of meaningless patterns. He gave them both kinds of pattern because he reasoned that children would use words to remember the meaningful patterns but not the meaningless ones. This then was his way of testing verbal memory. Whether or not it was a good test of verbal memory is an issue that need not detain us here. All that needs to be said is that there was a difference between the two groups with the meaningful figures – the poorer readers were worse at remembering them than the other children – but not with the meaningless ones. From this and similar results Bakker concluded that 'the retention of temporal order influences the reading – learning process', and he argued that it was memory for verbal material that was particularly important. In other words his was a causal hypothesis. Memory in his view determined reading: poor memory led to backward reading.

Do not be impressed by this conclusion. An alternative to it waits, quite plausibly, in the wings. The amount that children are able to remember changes as they grow older. For instance, the number of digits that children manage to remember in the Digit Span sub-test increases quite markedly as they grow older. We do not know all the reasons for this 'developmental' change, but one of the influences could well be the experience of learning to read. After all, reading does involve remembering words and sounds. The child who learns to read is constantly exercising his memory, and this of course could be one of the reasons why he is able to remember so much more as he grows older.

Exactly the same reason could account for the poor showing made by backward readers in tests of auditory memory. As unsuccessful readers they will have had much less of the sort of practice which we have just mentioned. If they cannot work out what any of the words in a sentence mean there is no need for them to remember anything about the sentence's beginning by the time they reach its end. It follows inexorably that their poor memory scores could just as well be the result as the source of the failure to learn to read.

Let us look at another more recent study which has the advantage of trying to isolate precisely what is wrong with the memory of backward readers. This is an American study conducted by David Holmes and William McKeever, who compared a group of 13-year-old 'dyslexics' with other 13-year-old children who had learned to read without any difficulty. Two kinds of material were used in the various tests of memory. In some tests the children had to remember written words, and in others photographs of faces. The experimenters made this comparison because they wanted to find out whether backward readers remember everything, or just words, badly. In fact they found that it was only the words that caused the backward readers any particular difficulty, and then only in tests where they had to remember what order the words came in.

This is an ingenious study in many ways with an interesting result. Differences as specific as this are hard to find and valuable when they are found. And it is not an isolated result. In 1982 Isabelle Liberman together with several colleagues at the Haskins Laboratory in America also took measures of how well children remember faces and words (in this case nonsense words) and they too found that poor readers were at no particular disadvantage when they had to remember the faces, but none the less were particularly forgetful with words.

Both sets of experimenters thought that they had demon-strated something specifically wrong with these children's memory. One of the reasons, they claimed, why backward readers fall behind in reading is that they cannot remember the words and sounds that they hear or see written down. But, of course, their experiments do not get round the cause–effect problem. The backward readers' very specific difficulty with remembering words could very well be a consequence of their slow progress in learning about written language.

One way round this problem is, as we mentioned in chapter 1, to mount a longitudinal study. We did this a few years ago and one of the measures that we took was of the children's ability to remember words. We saw 368 children over a period of four years, starting when they were four or five years old and could not yet read, and going on until they had reached the age of eight or nine and for the most part had made good progress in reading. We shall deal with three points in time during this four-year period.[5]

1    when we first saw them; one of the many tests which we gave them at this stage was a measure of their memory for words;

2    a year and a half later when they were seven years old. We measured their reading and spelling levels for the first time at this point;

3    when we saw them for the last time when they were

either eight or nine years old: one of the many tests that we administered was again a test of memory for words, slightly harder than the test given earlier but with just the same format. We also measured their memory for single numbers (digits), a common way of testing memory.

What should one expect from this study? Different things should happen if memory determines how well children read than if their success in reading determines how well they remember – our two alternatives. If memory affects reading – Jorm's idea – the memory scores at Point 1 should predict how well children read later on at Point 2. But they did not.

On the other hand, if reading experiences determine how well children remember, their reading levels at Point 2 should predict how well they remember later on at Point 3 – which they did. So it looks as though the hypothesis about memory deficits being a cause of reading failure must go the same way as the earlier ideas about perceptual weaknesses. It seems much more likely to be the other way round. Reading probably determines memory, and not memory reading.

But we still have to face a related question. It concerns learning. The experiments on memory simply involved presenting some material once only to the children. What happens when it is presented over and over again, and the children given the chance to learn it? In that case would backward readers be at a particular loss when they have to learn about verbal material? This is a question that has been asked by a number of people and most notably by Frank Vellutino. In fact his studies have provided some of the strongest arguments for the idea of a verbal deficit. Yet once again the evidence needs close questioning. All the studies make the traditional mental-age match.

Take an experiment by Vellutino and his colleagues. They looked at children of 9, 10 and 11 years, some of whom were backward readers while the rest read normally for their age. Half the children in each group had to learn to make associations between meaningless patterns and meaningless noises. The other half had to learn new names for particular patterns. The results were very clear. The backward readers learned the first task with meaningless material as well as the other children did, but were at a severe disadvantage in the second which involved new names. Vellutino and his colleagues argued quite convincingly that the difference was due to the second task being a verbal one. The backward reading group did have more difficulty learning verbal associations.

But this does not tell us what causes what. Cause and effect could go either way. Certainly failing to associate words with patterns could disrupt learning to read, and this seems to be Vellutino's idea of what happens. But equally poor progress in reading could hold back the child's success in making verbal associations. We cannot tell. There is no convincing evidence of a verbal deficit here.

## 'Decoding'

We are used to skills becoming automatic. When a child originally learns, say, to tie his shoe-laces he has to attend to every single movement if he is to be sure of getting the knot right. But several tied shoe-laces later he no longer has to follow what he is doing nearly so assiduously. His actions have become automatic. It is often suggested, and with some plausibility, that it is the same thing with several aspects of reading and writing. Words which originally have to be painfully deciphered are soon read so rapidly and automatically that the child has no idea any longer how he actually does work out their meaning. If one accepts this persuasive argument, it is a small step to asking the question whether this transition from conscious deciphering to easy automatic reading is as smooth among backward readers as it is with other children.

Several psychologists have suggested that herein lies a crucial difference between the two groups of children. The backward reader, they suggest, does not find it so easy to read words automatically and this is one of the main reasons for his difficulties. A good example of a study taking this view is the one by Charles Perfetti and Thomas Hogaboam, who work in Pittsburgh. Their technique was simplicity itself. They simply showed eight and ten-year-old children a set of words for a limited time and asked the children to read them. Some of the children had fallen behind in reading and others had not (an unfortunate aspect of this study was that the skilled readers were considerably more intelligent than the backward readers). Some of the words used were common ones: others were more unusual: still others were 'nonsense words', made-up words which meant nothing. Perfetti and Hogaboam timed how long it took the children to read each word.

The backward readers took longer to read the words: their relative slowness was more pronounced when they had to read the less common words and the nonsense words, but it was there, too, even with the common words. The experimenters' explanation was that these children were not reading automatically. To quote from the study: 'At least some unskilled comprehenders may have failed to develop automatic decoding skills and . . . this failure may lead to diminished comprehending skills'.

Two Dutch psychologists, H. Bouma and C.P. Legein, carried out a very similar project. They compared a group of backward readers aged from 11 to 15 years to other children of the same age, and showed the children letters or words, again measuring the time it took to read them. Once again the backward readers were considerably slower than the other children. The experimenters concluded that backward readers are particularly slow at translating visual information into speech, and that this slowness is a real problem for them.

Perhaps the best way to deal with studies like this – and it should be said that there are many – is to consider what else could have happened. Very little, is the answer. For, when the impressive terms are removed and the forbidding theories forgotten, one can see that *all that these studies show is that backward readers read poorly*. It would be surprising indeed if they had not been slower than the rest. After all, they were backward readers, and backward readers find it difficult to read. We do not need experiments to show that they fumble when they read. We knew that already.

This circular research is probably the most extreme example of the problem of the kind of comparison, the mental-age match, which troubles us. It makes no sense to go on and on showing that children who have problems with reading are worse on this or that measure than other children of the same age. Every single difference between the groups is bound to be ambiguous. Yet most analyses of 'dyslexia' and indeed most theories about the way children learn to read are founded on studies of this unhelpful form. It is this more than anything else that has led the subject astray, not just because the evidence is so ambiguous but also because there is so much of it. Too many 'differences' between backward readers have been found.

## Phonological awareness

Now we can turn to a topic where there is at last some convincing evidence for a genuine deficit which is responsible for some of the difficulties of the backward reader. It is a deficit in the child's awareness of the sounds which make up the words he hears and speaks.

To understand why this kind of awareness might be important we must turn to the alphabet. Alphabets work by breaking words up into small segments of sound and representing these sounds by letters. So, even a simple monosyllabic word like 'cat' is divided into the three sounds and written in the three letters: 'c', 'a', 't'. In fact at this level of analysis the number of sounds that we use in our language is rather small and that means that one needs relatively few letters to represent them. So the advantage of such a system is obvious: it is immensely economic, with twenty-four letters representing hundreds of thousands of words – which is, whichever way one looks at it, a very good bargain.

The idea of breaking up words into their component sounds seems such a simple one that it comes as a surprise that alphabetic scripts came rather late on the historical scene. They were preceded by pictograms, after which came logographic scripts in which each symbol represents a particular meaning. Logographic scripts still flourish – Chinese is one. They are the very antithesis of the alphabet. They are not at all economic: they contain an immense number of symbols which certainly tax the memories of both children and adults and which can only be learned over a long period of time. We once met an engineering student in Japan, who told us that he was still learning to read. This was not because he was in any way a slow reader, but simply because he was dealing with new concepts which were represented by symbols (one of the Japanese scripts is also logographic) which he had not come across before.

Historically the next kind of script to be invented was not the alphabet but the syllabary. Syllabaries have one crucial property in common with the alphabet. They too work by breaking words into component sounds, but here the unit of sound is rather a large one – the syllable. Each letter denotes a syllable; every syllable in the language is represented by a different letter. Although this system would be unspeakably prolific in English, which contains many syllables, it works extremely well for Japanese where there is a very small range of syllables.

The Japanese have a type of script called *kana*, in which there are only 36 letters each signifying an individual syllable. Rather confusingly they use two such syllabaries. The *kana* scripts are extremely regular, and apparently very easy to learn. Anyone who knows them can be sure of reading or writing any word in the language in these scripts – an achievement which is expected of schoolchildren by the age of eight. It may seem strange given such an effective system of reading and writing, but they choose to combine these syllabaries with another script called *kanji* which is logographic and which was imposed on them centuries ago by the Chinese. In principle any sentence in Japanese could be written entirely in one of their syllabic scripts. In practice this happens very rarely indeed, and looks distinctly odd to the

Japanese eye when it does. Virtually every written Japanese sentence consists of some words written in *kana* and others in *kanji*.[6]

The radical differences between logographic, syllabic and alphabetic scripts raise some fascinating questions for anyone interested in reading difficulties. We already have answers to some of these questions. For instance, we now know that the overall incidence of reading backwardness among children in Japan, in Chinese-speaking countries (in this case Taiwan) and in the West (the USA) is very similar.[7] There seems at the moment to be no case for saying that one kind of script is in the end more demanding and more difficult than another, although they do quite clearly make very different demands.

We shall return to the significance of the three kinds of script in a later chapter when we consider the relationship between reading and writing. For the present we need only note the crucial point that an alphabet is but one of several types of script, and that it makes its own characteristic demands. What are they?

The most obvious and indeed the most important is that it depends absolutely on the child being aware of the sounds in words. He must realize that simple and well-known words like 'cat' are made up of three segments – usually called phonemes – arranged in a certain order and that different segments or the same segments arranged in a different order would produce a different word. At first sight this seems an easy demand. After all, any child of three can hear and understand the difference between the words 'cat' and 'mat' or between 'cat' and 'cap', and these are pairs of words which differ in terms of one phoneme only. If children can make these distinctions, are they not aware of phonemes?

The answer to this question is 'not necessarily'. There are many examples of skills which we master, remaining all the while quite unaware of how we manage to do so. Riding a bicycle is one: try to remember how you manage not to fall over when your bicycle tilts slightly to the right. Your answer will almost certainly be wrong: you will say one thing, the wrong thing, and do another. Crawling is an even simpler example. The great developmental psychologist Piaget once asked an audience of distinguished academics to sketch on a piece of paper the successive relative positions that would be taken by their hands and knees if they were to crawl from one part of a room to another. Their answers were spectacularly wrong.[8]

So children might at first be completely unaware of the existence of the segments of sound in words. This is an idea to which many people hold. The idea in full is that the most important aspect of speech for the young child is its meaning, and its meaning is contained in words and sentences. Words and sentences then are what she is most aware of, and though of course she relies on minute differences in sounds to discern the words' meanings, she is not particularly aware of doing so, just as we are not particularly aware of the precise movements which keep us aloft on our bicycles. In fact, the argument continues, it is only when children begin to learn to read that they start to think about the sounds within words. The child has to be taught how to spot the component sounds in words before he can read properly and even more certainly before he can spell with any accuracy at all.

The argument is applied to the question of difficulties in reading. One common development of the argument is that it is at this stage that backward readers are particularly vulnerable. For some reason, usually not given, they find it especially hard to rise to this new awareness. Words remain words to them – indivisible and impenetrable. Let us look at the evidence for this hypothesis.

First there are reports that young children without much experience in reading find tasks which demand some form of phonological awareness impossibly difficult. One very famous study of this sort was done in Cambridge by D.J. Bruce. He devised an ingenious task, called a subtraction task. He read out words to children whose mental ages went from five years to just over nine years and asked them to imagine what each word would sound like, if a particular sound were taken away from it – for example, what the word 'stand' would be like without the 't' sound, or 'left' without its 'f'. This was a difficult task particularly for the younger children, and it was only children of eight years or more who managed to solve it consistently.

Bruce concluded that awareness of sounds in words is something which comes remarkably late in childhood. This was also the conclusion reached by several psychologists in America. The Haskins Laboratory, a centre well known for its work on speech and hearing, was responsible for the famous 'tapping' experiment. In this experiment, children were given a stylus and had to tap with it every time a word was read out to them. They were, in fact, given two of these tapping tasks, a 'phoneme' and a 'syllable' task. In the phoneme task the children had to learn to tap out the number of phonemes in each word, so that three taps to the word 'cat' and four to 'sand' would here be the correct responses. In the syllable task they had to tap out the number of syllables – for example, two to the word 'many' and three to 'remember'.

The phoneme task was very much the more difficult of the two, and usually impossible for children who had not yet begun to read. Once again the investigators' conclusion was that children are not aware of phonemes until they begin to learn to read.

Together Bruce's experiment and the Haskin's study look decidedly impressive. But one must be cautious. Both the difficult tasks – phoneme subtraction and tapping out phonemes – make other demands on the children as well as asking them to be aware of particular sounds. Phoneme subtraction after all involves subtraction – always a difficult manouevre for young children. Tapping involves rhythm and the rhythm of a word is plainly captured in its syllables and not in its phonemes. So in one case the children might have failed because they did not really understand what they had to do and in the other they may have been misled by the rhythmic nature of the task.

People who have never had the opportunity to learn to read and write are our second source of evidence. They are important simply because they should not be blessed with any ability which depends on learning to read. So, if we only become aware of phonemes through the experience of learning to read, illiterate people should not be aware of them at all. Illiteracy is comparatively rare in our society, but it is commoner in others. Portugal is one place where illiterate people can still be found in appreciable numbers, and it was there that an influential study on awareness of sounds in illiterate people was done. Jõse Morais and a group of his colleagues based in Brussels carried out this project.

They went to a poor rural area and gathered together two groups, one of literate and another of illiterate adults. These groups, the research workers claimed, were like each other in every respect apart from the fact that one could read whereas the other could not. In fact, many of the literate group had only begun to read as the result of literacy programmes introduced by the army or by industry. The experimenters set out to measure these people's awareness of sounds with tests similar to those used by Bruce. One actually involved the subtraction of a sound. The people, literate and illiterate alike, were asked, for example, what the word 'purso' would sound like without the 'p' (the answer 'urso' means a bear in Portuguese). In another test a sound had to be added: to take one example, the experimenter would ask what 'allacho' would sound like with an exra 'p' at its beginning (the answer in this case means a 'clown').

The aim of the experiment was to see if people who have not had the experience of learning to read are at a disadvantage with tasks like these. It turned out that there was a clear difference between the two groups. The illiterates made many more errors than the others. The illiterate group only managed to produce the right answer 21 per cent of the time, whereas the literate group managed to be right with 72 per cent of the words. Naturally Morais and his colleagues concluded that awareness of the constituent sounds in words is a direct result of being taught how to read. Reading, according to them, produces the awareness and not the other way round.

It is an impressive result, but one should be a little cautious.

We cannot conclude from it that *all* phonological awareness comes after, and as a consequence of, learning to read. The addition or subtraction of a sound is just one of many possible ways of testing people's awareness of sounds, and it is quite possible that people who are not at all good at this task nevertheless do in some way know how words can be broken into smaller segments of sound.

Indeed when one thinks further about it the claims made by Morais and his colleagues take on an extravagant air. Many of the commonest routines in life seem to demand considerable attention to sounds, and these demands apply to illiterate people just as much as they do to anyone else. Rhymes are the most obvious and possibly the most important example. When someone realizes that two words rhyme he is to some extent dissecting the sounds of those words. As soon as he knows that 'cat' and 'hat' have a sound in common and that the sound is '-at' he has broken up each of the two words into smaller units of sound. It is a fairly crude dissection, as the detached segment '-at' counts as a syllable. Nevertheless the child who understands rhyme must know something about the constituent sounds of words.

Nursery rhymes are a staple part of children's early lives, and this is probably as true of Portugal as it is of anywhere else. It is hard to believe that illiterate people never appreciate rhyme.[9] Many of Chaucer's audiences must have been illiterate. Did they never appreciate the rhymes when they heard:

> "Took her in his armes two and kiste her ofte,
> And her to glade he di al his entente,
> For which her goost, that flickered all alofte,
> Into her woful herte again it wente".
> (*Troilus and Criseyde*)

If illiterates perceive and like rhymes, so apparently do young children. They give every appearance of enjoying nursery rhymes and jingles which involve rhymes and they seem to remember them well. Their attention is captured by simple games and routines in which rhyming words play a great part ('Round and round the garden' for example). If they take in the rhymes, they must in some sense also be aware of speech sounds. And since we are talking about very young children – children who are nowhere near beginning to read – we are implying that, contrary to all the experimenters we have mentioned so far, this sort of awareness precedes reading by a very significant period of time.

So the obvious next step is to see whether it is true that young children do appreciate rhyme and to find out how well they do so. There is still remarkably little evidence to answer this question. Some of the most striking of the evidence that does exist comes from informal observations. For example, Dan Slobin, a leading psycholinguist, reports that his three-year-old daughter made the following striking remarks: 'Eggs are deggs. Enough-duff. More-bore'. She was obviously attending to the words' constituent sounds when she said these things. Many other examples of the same kind of attention are to be found in the justly famous book '*From Two to Five*' by Kornei Chukovsky, a Russian educationalist. It is full of examples of neatly rhyming poems created, with evident relish, by very young children. Here are six of them, made up by three- and four-year-old children.

> Give me, give me, before I die
> Lots and lots of potato pie
>
> I'm a whale.
> This is my tail
>
> I'm a big, big rider
> You're smaller than a spider.
>
> I'm a flamingo
> Look at my wingo
>
> The red house
> Made of strouss
>
> The duckling and the big goose
> Sat on the broken sail-oose

This last verse certainly is a dramatic example of the importance of rhyme to young children. Not only does the two-and-a-half-year-old child recognize rhyme and produce rhyming sentences with ease: she also changes the very form of words which she knows to suit the rules of rhyme. It is quite plain that all these children know a great deal about how to spot the common sounds in different words. They show this every time that they produce a rhyme.

They show it too when they detect rhymes. We now have good experimental evidence that they can do this as well. Charles Read had quite striking success with four-year-old children when he gave them an amusing rhyming game. It involved puppets with particular names: these puppets liked words which rhymed with their names ('Would Ed like bed or bead?' 'food or fed?'). Most of the kindergarten children in the study managed to play this game with very little difficulty.

This quite remarkable achievement on the part of young children has been all but ignored by child psychologists, who on the whole are more interested in children's gaffes than in their triumphs. Nevertheless it seems fair to assume that children are aware of rhymes, dabble in them, enjoy them and probably learn a great deal from them about the phonological structure of their language – and all this long before they go to school. And it is surely a reasonable suggestion that these experiences might later on have an effect on how well these children come to terms with the alphabet. Chukovsky probably had this in mind when he made this striking statement about the importance of children's rhymes:

> Rhyme-making during the second year of life is an inescapable stage of our linguistic development. Children who do not perform such linguistic exercises are abnormal or ill. These activities are indeed exercises, and it is difficult to think of a more rational system in phonetics than such frequent repetition of all possible sound variations.

This brings us rather sharply back to reading problems. We have mentioned some definite signs of an active interest in sounds in most children long before they learn to read. Now we need to know whether those who for one reason or another remain relatively insensitive to rhymes and uninterested in them are, as a result, more likely to become backward readers. Do the causal links run that way?

Once again we are faced with surprisingly little evidence. There are studies which show a relationship between children's reading levels and their sensitivity to rhyme clearly enough, but they used the traditional mental-age match, and so we cannot assume anything about causes from the results of these studies.

But there is one study on rhyming which does use the more convincing reading-age match. The great advantage of this design, as we have seen, is that it rules out the possibility that any difference which emerges between normal and backward readers is the product of a discrepancy in reading levels, since: the reading levels are the same. We ourselves carried out a study of this sort several years ago.[10] We saw a large group of backward readers, all of whom were in normal schools, and whose intelligence levels were average or above. No clear evidence existed that any of their learning difficulties were the product of emotional, physical or social handicaps. We compared them with a younger group of children who read normally for their age and whose reading levels were the same as those of the backward reading group.

We gave all the children two types of task. One involved detecting rhyme and alliteration, and the other producing rhyme. In the detection task we said four words at a time, all but one of which shared a common sound, and the child's task was to spot that word. Sometimes the common sound which the odd word did not share was the opening consonant (e.g. 'sun, sea, sock, rag'), sometimes the middle vowel ('nod, red, fed, bed'), and sometimes the end consonant ('weed, peel, need, deed'). Notice that the first of these three conditions deals in alliteration, and the other two in rhyme. In the production task we simply read out a series of words to each child, and asked the child after saying each word to think of another one which rhymed with it.

The backward readers did not fare at all well. Despite the fact that they were older and more advanced intellectually, and despite the fact that both tests involved only spoken words, their scores were a great deal worse than those of the normal readers – between three and six times worse in the three tasks. The test of alliteration was generally the hardest of the three, and it put the backward readers at a particular disadvantage in comparison to the other children. We shall have more to say about alliteration in later chapters.

So here, at last, we have evidence for a definite and a specific deficit among children who are in difficulty with reading. Many of them are quite remarkably insensitive to rhyme, and it would be hard to claim that this insensitivity is the result of their reading problem. They could read as well as the other children, and yet were far behind in working out whether words rhymed or not. There is no reason here for thinking that reading determines awareness of sounds. It looks as if the cause–effect relationship goes the other way round. These children's insensitivity to sounds may well have been one of the main reasons for the difficulties which they encountered as soon as they began to learn to read.

Obviously this is an important conclusion, but we cannot leave it there. If we are right, the backward readers' insensitivity to the sounds in speech should show up in the kind of mistakes that they make when they do try to read and write. This gives us a way of looking at these mistakes. Another implication of what we have been saying is that measures of children's sensitivity to rhyme taken *before* they go to school should predict how well they learn to read *after* they get there. But the last and most important consequence of our claims is a practical one. Teaching children to be aware of rhyme should help them learn to read and write, and it should be a particular help to those children who are struggling with learning to read. Here then is our first educational suggestion, and we shall deal with it more fully in the next chapter.

Notes

1 We are referring here to the work by Isabelle Liberman and her colleagues (1971) on normal children and by Lyle (1969) and Holmes and Pepper (1977) on backward readers.

2 For a fuller discussion of the question of children's perception of mirror image figures see *Perception and Understanding in Young Children* by Peter Bryant (1974).

3 Leslie Henderson's interesting book (1982) sets out the criticisms of this idea very clearly and comprehensively.

4 These and other experiments on the question of reading and intermodal connections are reviewed in a chapter by Peter Bryant in a book edited by D.D. Duane and M.B. Rawson (1975). Frank Vellutino's book (1979) also contains a full account of this work.

5 The first description of this project was in a paper that we published in 1983 in *Nature*. In 1985 we published a detailed monograph, called *Rhyme and Reason in Reading and Spelling*, which sets out our methods in the project in detail.

6 The clearest account of the history of different scripts is to be found in the justly famous book by I.J. Gelb, *A Study of Writing* (1963).

7 It was thought at one time that few or no Japanese children suffered unexpected difficulties with reading, but the work by Harold Stevenson and his colleagues (1982) seems to contradict this.

8 The best account of these ideas is in Piaget's *The Grasp of Consciousness* (1978).

9 We and the Brussels team have been engaged in a friendly controversy on the question of the direction of cause and effect *vis à vis* learning to read and phonological awareness. See the note by Bertelson and his colleagues and our reply to it in *Nature*, 1985.

10 The work is described in our paper in *Nature*, 1978.

# 4

# Awareness of sounds and reading

The discovery that backward readers are very poor at detecting rhyme or alliteration prompts two questions. One is whether this particular skill is an important one for every child. If it is, one would expect children who are, for example, particularly good at rhyming to become excellent readers. The second question is about the nature of the skill. Are backward readers poor only with rhyme or do they fail at any test of awareness of sounds in words?

## How widespread are the effects of the skill?

The question is clear enough, and there seems to be no problem about how to find an answer: simply see how well a large group of children copes with a task in which they have to respond to segments of sounds in words and then look at the relationship between that and how well they learn to read. The only important decision is about the age at which you begin to test the children.

This too is easily settled. There are very good arguments for starting young – for measuring their sensitivity to sounds before they begin to read. We gave the reason for this in the first chapter. If $A$ causes $B$, $A$ should also precede $B$. If the children's ability to see that different words have common sounds does affect their reading, then their success in reading should be influenced by how sensitive they became to sounds *before* learning to read. Any measure of this skill in a large group of pre-school children should be related to how well they read in later years.

There is another, more practical reason for starting young: it concerns the neglected question of prevention. As we showed in the last chapter, the kind of activity over which backward readers stumble so badly is actually a commonplace of early childhood. Long before they go to school, children play word-games and make up rhymes: yet rhyming is remarkably difficult for backward readers. This suggests in turn that the seeds, or at least some of the seeds, of reading failure may be sown long before the child goes to school. It may go back to the time – say at three or four years of age – when children are normally getting interested in word-games and in nursery rhymes. That could be when things begin to go wrong, and that could also be the time when precautionary steps could and should be taken. These might stop children from ever becoming backward readers by making sure that they have these experiences and have them successfully.

So the next step is to look at children before they go to school and see what relationship there is between (1) what they are like then, and (2) how well they cope with reading and writing in later years. For this, we must look at longitudinal studies. What is the best way to test our theory in a longitudinal study? Obviously we ought to see if there is a relationship between early skills with speech sounds and eventual success with reading. The more skilled the child is with things like rhymes early on, the better his reading and writing should be later. But one needs a more stringent test than that. This relationship should exist even when allowances are made for intelligence. It would be no surprise if the brightest children turned out to be good at rhyming at four years and good at reading as well when they are, say, eight years old. The bright child might simply be doing both things well because he is bright. The crucial thing is to show that this relationship exists even *when intelligence is held constant* and comparisons are made between children of equal intelligence.

There are several longitudinal studies which fit this bill. In the studies which we are going to describe, the children were

tested on various skills before they went to school and then
their progress in reading and sometimes in other skills as well
were measured over several school years. We shall confine
ourselves to three such studies, one done in Sweden, one in
America and the third by us in England, because they seemed
to be the most comprehensive and the most convincing. There
are others, but they led to much the same conclusion as the
ones which we shall describe.

Ingvar Lundberg and his colleagues were responsible for
the Swedish study, which started with 200 six-to-seven-year-
old kindergarten children who were tested for the first time a
few months before starting school. It ended a year and a half
later by which time 143 of the original group were still being
studied.[1] (One expects something of a drop-out in projects
which last for some time, but the loss of over a quarter of the
children in this case is rather high.)

When they were first seen the children were given a large
number of tests, many of which measured their ability to
segment speech sounds. One, of particular interest to our
argument, involved rhyme. An adult said eight words, and
each time the child had to think of another word which
rhymed with the one which he had just heard. In other tasks
the child had to say what particular words would sound like if
their phonemes were reversed, to break words up into
syllables and, in another test, into phonemes, and to identify
the position of particular sounds like 's' in words read out to
him. One year later when the group – by now fully fledged
schoolchildren – were visited at their school, they were given
reading and spelling tests and their linguistic skills were
measured as well. Thus the central aim of this study was to
look for a relationship between the kindergarten child's
awareness of sounds and his progress at school a year later
(and then again after another six-month period) in learning to
read and spell.

By and large the study was successful. The children who
did well in the initial tests of awareness of sounds were also the
ones who made most progress in learning to read at school.
This is quite an impressive result given that the children had

only been at school for rather less than eighteen months when the study came to its end, and also that the relationships held even when the children's intelligence was taken into account.

But the study did leave one rather worrying gap. The only educational skills measured in the second half of the study were reading and spelling. This is not enough. The theory is about a highly specific connection, a specific link between a child's early experience with the sounds in words and his later success with the alphabet and through that with reading. There is no room in the theory for a similar relation between this pre-school skill and some other educational skill like mathematics. Segmentation of sounds should affect reading but not mathematics. The Swedish study did not check this in any way. It may seem churlish to say so in the face of such clear cut results, but they should have tested mathematics (or some other educational skill) and shown that there was a much stronger connection between the original pre-school measures and reading or spelling than there was between these measures and mathematics. However, the study's results are certainly consistent with the idea of a link between the child's ability to disentangle the sounds in words and his later progress in learning to read: but that link is still not firmly established.

The second study was reported in 1983 by Barbara Fox and Donald Routh. It added one new item of information of great interest: that if a child has difficulty with analysing speech sounds at the age of six, he is likely to be reading and spelling poorly three years later even though the actual difficulty with sounds has long since passed. Fox and Routh looked at 20 children, first when they were six after one year at school and later when they were nine. Ten of these children had already been diagnosed as backward readers by the time that the project began, and Fox and Routh showed that at that time these particular children failed miserably on a test which measured how well they could break up syllables into their constituent phonemes. The other ten children made no mistakes at all in this test.

Three years later the backward readers had got over this

difficulty with the test of analysing speech sounds. But their reading and spelling had fallen even further behind, and their spelling mistakes tended to be, to use the experimenters' own term, 'bizarre'. By this they meant that the alphabetic letters that the backward readers wrote often had little relation to the actual sounds of the word they were trying to spell. Fox and Routh concluded that the early difficulty with sounds had had lasting effects and that these still played a considerable part in the children's spelling, even though the original weakness had itself disappeared.

It is an interesting piece of work, but it also has its difficulties. It has one problem in common with the Swedish study, the only educational tests at the end being tests of reading and spelling: once again we cannot be sure that the children's early difficulties with speech sounds were specifically related to reading and spelling. On top of this, the number of children in the study was extremely small, and anyway the whole project started after children had begun to be taught to read (remember that the backward readers were known as such when the study started). We cannot be sure that we are studying the influence of a skill acquired before school.

We turn now to our longitudinal study.[2] It was a project which lasted longer than either of the other two projects and involved many more children. It also checked that the connection between the children's early skills and their progress later on was specific to reading. It was more than just a longitudinal study, as it combined a longitudinal study with training.

We shall deal with the longitudinal part first. We started with 400 children, aged four to five years. The four-year-olds were all at nursery schools and the five-year-olds in their first term at school. Earlier we had made sure that none of them could read, and indeed we had rejected any child (there were about 100 of them) who had shown any sign of reading any words at all. The first stage was to give them a series of rhyming and alliteration tasks which were very similar to those we had given the backward readers in our earlier study which we described at the end of chapter 2. We said three or four words at a time (three to the four-year olds and four to the five-year olds) all but one of which had a sound in common. The child had to listen to the words and tell us which was the odd one out. We also varied the position of the crucial sound in the words. In some cases it was at the end (e.g. bun *hut* gun sun), in others in the middle (e.g. *hug* pig dig wig), and in the rest at the beginning (bud bun bus *rug*). In the first two cases the children had to spot which words rhymed: in the third they had to be aware of alliteration. At the same time we measured the children's verbal intelligence and their memory. We were then in a position to measure the connection between these scores and the children's progress at school.

The study went on for another four years when the children had reached the age of eight or nine years. In fact a great deal else went on between the initial and final tests: we took many measures during that time. But here we shall concentrate on the final tests, which measured how intelligent the children were and how well they could read and spell and, as an essential extra check, solve mathematical problems.

Our results were resoundingly positive. The children's scores on the initial rhyming tests did predict their progress in reading and spelling three or four years later on, and did so very well. The relationship stood up even when we removed the effects of differences in intelligence. There was a new twist too: the childen's early rhyming scores did not seem to bear any relation to their success in mathematics. So here is good evidence that the link between rhyming and learning to read and spell is a specific one. It is also a connection which remains strong for as long as three years. It must be important.

There is one more thing to be said here about our longitudinal results and this concerns the differences between the test which dealt with the first sound of each word (alliteration) and the other tests which involved the middle vowel sounds and the end consonant (rhyme). We have only talked about the latter tests, so let us turn now to alliteration.

We found that it was quite significantly harder both for the four- and for the five-year-olds than were the tests which dealt with rhyme. This is rather interesting since on the face of it all three tests seem to measure the same skill – categorizing words by common sounds. But the early experience which children have with categorizing words in this way tends to be with rhyme rather than with alliteration. Rhyme is the stuff of word-games and, of course, of nursery rhymes. So interestingly enough the difference suggests that we are dealing with a skill which really is affected by experience. Children have experience with rhymes and are better at them. And as we have seen the skill which they acquire is related to the way they read years later. All this suggests that not only early skills but also early experiences with speech sounds have a lasting and important effect.

Now we can return to the question whether there is a genuine continuum. Our results suggest, strongly and unambiguously, that there is. The skill which backward readers lack seems to play its part right through the range of success and failure in reading. The better endowed the child is with this skill, the more likely it is that his reading will surpass expectations, and vice versa. This is something which concerns more than the minority group of children whom we call backward readers. It is important to every child. There is nothing here to support the idea of a separate and distinct group of backward readers and a great deal to suggest that such a group might not exist.


## Improving the skill

When a skill turns out to be of such importance one begins to wonder whether there are ways of improving it. Doing so might well help children to read. But there is another important reason too for wondering about the effects of training. Suppose that we found ways of teaching children to be more aware of rhyme and alliteration, and suppose, too, that we showed that, purely as a result of this teaching,

children were also able to read better. This happy set of
results would clinch the argument that a child's skill with
sounds in words does affect – does, in other words, have a
causal influence on – his progress in learning to read. In
chapter 2 we set out the reasons why combining longitudinal
studies with training is the only convincing way to demonstrate that one thing causes another in a child's development.

Fortunately many people have studied ways of teaching
children to be aware of speech sounds. Most of the studies
have in different ways been extremely successful. Here we
shall describe some of the projects which dealt with training
phonological skills and with learning to read.

In 1976 David Fox and Barbara Routh showed that it was
quite possible to teach even children as young as four to
'blend' sounds. In a blending task the child hears several
sounds (e.g. 'c', 'a', 't') and has to work out what word they
make. It is, in one way, an auditory analogy of reading words
letter by letter which involves blending the sounds typical of
each letter. The Fox/Routh study demonstrated that one can
improve young children's skill at putting sounds together in
quite a short time – two sessions in fact. The adult
experimenter simply demonstrated blending, starting with
five 'two-sound' words – words like 'me', 'say' and 'way'.
After that the child himself had first to listen to two sounds
and then to blend them in the same way. He did this several
times and was told each time whether he was right or not. The
fact that the children could do this in itself is an interesting
observation, but the next part of the experiment was more
interesting. To the children who had had this training and to
others who had not they gave another task, very like reading,
in which children first had to associate particular shapes like
$\Delta$ and $\Psi$ with sounds like 'm' and 'ay' and then had to work
out what word pairs of patterns indicated. Using the shapes
and sounds just mentioned, the pair $\Delta\Psi$ would come out as
'may'. The experimenters wanted to know whether the
children who had been taught to blend sounds would be better
at this reading-like task than the rest. They were, but they
only seemed to benefit if they had, at the beginning of the

study, shown some knowledge of the way in which words can be broken into sounds.

This was an important study, but marred slightly by the rather artificial nature of the final test. One cannot be sure that reading off strings of patterns is directly related to the way children read real words. None the less the results do suggest that teaching children how to handle sounds could help them when they begin to learn to read.

Let us turn now to a project conducted by Joanna Williams which looked at the effect of training on children who are at school and have already begun to learn to read. She studied a large number of children in New York between the ages of 7 and 12, whose level of intelligence was on the low side (an average IQ of 83). She gave over half of these children intensive training in how to deal with the component sounds in words. They were taught over a period of 18 weeks in lessons which occurred two to three times a week how to identify the beginning, middle and end sounds of monosyllabic words and also, as in Fox and Routh's study, how to blend sounds. The teachers used games and worksheets to teach the children about speech sounds. The rest of the children were given no training at all.

Now we turn to the effects on reading. Again the measure was somewhat artificial. The children had to read nonsense words which as we have seen make strong demands on children's knowledge of letter-sound correspondences – which of course was what the training was about – but may be read in rather different ways than real words. It is difficult to understand the reason for this unnecessary limitation in the New York study. Real words should have been used too.

Nevertheless the results are interesting. All the children were taught to read and to recognize particular nonsense words and later were asked in what was called a 'transfer test' to read other nonsense words which were made up of the sounds and letters in the original list but in different combinations. Once again the children who had been taught to handle speech sounds did better in the final reading tasks. They learned to read the first lot of nonsense words more rapidly and they fared a great deal better when the time came to read the new transfer list. It looks as though teaching children how to disentangle the sounds in words does help them to read.

But we have to remember that the children had to read single, nonsense words. We are still a long way from finding out about the effects on children reading meaningful words or sentences. And there is another serious problem with this and with many other training studies including the one done by Fox and Routh. Both the studies which we have described compared two groups of children, one trained to cope with speech sounds, and the other not trained at all. But this is not a fair comparison. The trouble is that the children who are taught to handle sounds inevitably experience at the same time a number of other quite extraneous things which do not happen to the 'control' group of children. The children who are taught get a great deal more attention: they also have the advantage of being given the new, special treatment which must encourage them and perhaps discourage the children who were not taught and therefore received none of this attention. So if at the end of the project the children who have been taught about sounds in words are better at reading than the other children, this difference may have nothing to do with the training in speech sounds.

Putting these two points together, we can see now that there is a need for a study which really does measure children's progress in reading and in which the control group is given exactly the same amount of attention and the same kind of experiences as the children taught to segment sounds apart from the crucial experience of dealing with the segments of sound.

Until recently the only study to meet these requirements was an experiment conducted by David Goldstein in America. He studied four-year-old children, and one of the reasons why his was such an interesting project is that it did show that one can do a great deal to prepare young children for reading. The children were all bright: their average mental age was five and a half, one full year ahead of their actual age. Goldstein's interest was in what he called the 'analysis and synthesis' of sounds and words. By 'synthesis' he meant blending, and by 'analysis' he meant the opposite – breaking a word down into its constituent sounds. Goldstein devised a test of these two things, and started his project by administering it and a test of memory to all 23 children. Then he divided them into two groups, an experimental and a control group.

This time the control group was a real control group. Goldstein took care to teach *both* groups. He gave all the children exactly the same material, in the same book, for the same amount of time. He just taught the two groups different things. He taught the children in the experimental group about the sounds and about the letter–sound correspondence in each word in the book. In contrast the children in the control group were taught about the names and the order of the letters in the same words. The teaching went on for thirteen weeks. At the end Goldstein gave all the children a reading test which he had constructed himself. It consisted partly of words in the book which he had used for teaching and partly of new words.

For our purposes the most important result was an appreciable difference in the way the children in the two groups managed the reading test. Those who had been trained about sounds fared considerably better than the children in the control group. Once again, and this time it looks convincing, children read better after being taught about sounds. One other comforting result – comforting because it agrees with some of the longitudinal studies mentioned earlier in this chapter – was a relation between how well children did in the original tests of analysis and synthesis and how well they could read words by the end of the project. The better they were at one, the more progess they made in the other.

Though this was a carefully designed project it too had its problems. One was its size. Too few children, drawn from too limited a part of the IQ range, and taught for too short a period (13 weeks is short in comparison to the time children normally spend learning how to read): all this means that it is difficult to be sure that the results have any general value.

It had one other major weakness, a weakness which it shares with most other such studies and which we have already mentioned when discussing longitudinal studies. Goldstein's final measures were of reading only. He should also have given other educational tests, tests of mathematical skills for example, to check that the effects of the training were specific to reading. It is not enough to be told that an improvement in awareness of sounds is followed by an improvement in reading. We want to be sure that reading improves more than, say, the ability to do sums.

We ourselves have done a study which, we think, fills these two gaps.[3] When we did the large-scale longitudinal study, described earlier in this chapter, we also looked at the effects of teaching children about rhyme and alliteration. We got together a group of 65 children who were 6 years old when the training began and, since it continued for two years, eight when it ended. We divided these children into four groups. We taught one group (Group I) about rhyme and alliteration. Our way of doing this was based closely on Lynette Bradley's experience as a teacher.[4] The children were shown a series of pictures of familiar objects: the names of all but one of them in each series had a sound in common. Each child went through 40 sessions, spread out over the two-year period, and as time went on the tasks became more and more sophisticated. But they were all designed to show the child that the words, which were the names of the pictures in front of them, had sounds in common. The photograph on page 64 shows the kind of material that we used. We shall describe this sort of teaching in more detail in our last chapter which deals with ways of teaching reading. For the moment the important point is that these children were taught about rhyme and alliteration and about nothing else.

Nothing like reading was involved in the training which the children in Group I received. No alphabetic letters and certainly no written words played any part in their experiences with us. However in the case of the next group (Group II) we made the connection with reading a great deal more explicit. During the first year of the study we treated the

*The child selected the pictures with names which had sounds in common. In this instance the words were bat, mat, hat and rat.*

children in this group in exactly the same way as we did Group I, but in the second year things changed. Now we also showed them plastic letters, and taught them to identify the sounds which the names of the pictures had in common with particular letters ('c' for 'cat' and 'cup'). The children used the plastic letters to form one word, then another and so on. As before, all the words in the series had a sound, or more than one sound, in common. We took care to emphasize the common sounds with the help of the appropriate plastic letters. As we finished with one word the child broke it up, but always left untouched the letter representing the sound which this word shared with the next: new letters were added to it to form the next word, and then the whole process was repeated again several times. The photograph gives an idea of how this was done. Our aim was to make the relationship between the shared sounds and the letters which represent them very obvious. Alliteration and rhyme, we hoped, would become literally tangible.

*The plastic letters allow the teacher to demonstrate in a striking way how words which have sounds in common often have clusters of letters in common.*

We needed a proper control group and not just one given no training at all. Since both the groups which we have dealt with so far learned how to categorize the pictures (on the basis of their sounds) we decided to teach the third (Group III) to categorize exactly the same pictures, but in a different way. They had to put them into conceptual categories (for example, things one finds in the kitchen, or animals). Thus these children were seen as often and received as much training in putting pictures – the same pictures – into categories. But they were not taught about speech sounds. Finally we did include another group of children (Group IV) who were not taught at all.

We wanted, of course, to see whether the experience of being taught to categorize words by their sounds (as were the first two groups) would improve the children's reading and spelling. So at the end of the project we gave the children standardized tests of reading and spelling. We gave them other tests as well, for example a maths test, as we had to check that we were having a specific effect on reading and spelling rather than a broad effect on educational progress in general.

We found that the two groups of children who were taught about categorizing words by their sounds were better readers and spellers than the ones who were taught to put words into conceptual categories. And the improvement was quite specific to reading and spelling, for in the mathematics test the difference between the first two groups and the rest was much smaller. Improving children's sensitivity to the sounds within words does have a strong and specific effect on their reading and spelling. At last we had good evidence for a definite causal connection. Measures of children's sensitivity to rhyme and alliteration predict their progress in reading, and teaching them about rhyme and alliteration enhances that progress.

But these results do more than establish a cause. They have considerable practical implications too. One striking thing about our study was how well the group of children did who were taught to categorize sounds *and* to represent these sounds with letters. Reading levels of six months better than the children just taught to categorize sounds, ten months better than those taught to categorize conceptually, and a full fourteen months better than those who received no training at all – these are very considerable differences and argue that we have found Bradley's method to be a powerful one. Why does it work so well?

We can only speculate, but our feeling is that the plastic letters allow the teacher to demonstrate in a striking way how words, which have sounds in common, also (often) have clusters of letters in common. When the teacher changes the word 'cat' to 'hat' (pointing out at the same time that these two words rhyme) she leaves the letters which represent the rhyming sound '-at' intact and simply subtracts 'c' and replaces it with 'h'. The element which changes (in this case the first letter) represents the difference between the two words. The element which remains represents what they have in common. We think that this brings home to the child how sets of words which have sounds in common often share spelling patterns as well.

This is a point which we shall discuss in more detail in our final two chapters on teaching. In the meantime we are pleased to have established how well this method of teaching children about speech sounds and their relation to alphabetic letters works, whatever the reason for its success.

## The importance of rhyme and of alliteration

Our chief concern in the study which we have just described was with children's sensitivity to rhyme and alliteration. We based our predictive measures on it, and we taught it as well. So far we have simply talked about this sensitivity as a measure of children's skills at handling the sounds in words, and that is what we believe it to be. But it seems to us that two skills, both directly relevant to reading, may be involved. One is to work out the sounds in words. The other is to put words into categories: these categories are of words ('cat', 'hat', 'mat', 'sat'; 'sound', 'found', 'pound') which share a common sound.

We have already said a great deal about the first skill. But the second could be as important. It is probably a very short intellectual step from knowing that 'light', 'fight', 'sight', and 'tight' all end in the same sound, to understanding that that is why they all also share a common spelling pattern. We are now stepping beyond the single letter–sound relationship and it is important that we should do so, because on the whole the connection between sequences of letters and sounds is a great deal more reliable than it is between single letters and sounds. The single letter 'i' signifies many different sounds in different words: the sequence '-ight' in contrast is a great deal more reliable.

We are speculating now because little is yet known about the connection between putting words into sound categories (rhyme and alliteration) and putting them into spelling categories (words which share the same spelling patterns). This is probably because we know very little anyway about the way in which children form this second kind of category.

Most of the suggestions made by psychologists have been negative. For example, George Marsh, a psychologist in California, has shown that children find it hard to use what they know about the spelling of a word like 'station' in order to work out how to spell or how to read an entirely new and made-up word like 'jation'. They do not at first, he concludes, make 'analogies': by this he means that they do not use the simple strategy of deciding that because two words sound the same they may be spelled in the same way, or that because two words are spelled in the same way they may sound the same.

However, words as strange as 'jation' could very well throw young children off their stroke. Why not try to answer the question using real words? That is what Usha Goswami, working in Oxford, has done recently, and with exciting as yet unpublished results. To take just one of a series of experiments, she showed six-year-old children a word which they could not read like 'beak', told them what it meant and then asked them to read other words. Some of these – 'bean', 'peak' – shared the same spelling patterns and also had a sound in common with the original word: others did not. She found that many young children could use the spelling pattern of one word to help them decipher other words, and could do so even though they had hardly begun to read. So, this kind of analogy is not something that comes late in reading. We think that it ought to be harnessed.

Of course this encouraging result itself raises new questions. Can backward readers make this kind of analogy? We can make the inference that they should find it particularly difficult to do so. After all, going from 'beak' to 'peak' depends on knowing that the two words rhyme, and that is precisely the thing that backward readers find very difficult. This means that the ability which Usha Goswami showed to come so early and so easily to the normal run of children, might very well elude many poor readers. That, of course, would have dire consequences, for it would put the backward reader at a pronounced disadvantage when he has to work out the meaning of written words that are new to him. It would also mean that he would be less likely than other children to see why groups of words like 'light' and 'fight' do have spelling patterns in common. The question can be settled easily enough by giving Usha Goswami's task to backward readers.

Suppose, for the moment, that we are right and that they would find the task particularly difficult. Then the next question would be how to teach them this. How does one show them how to form these categories and how to make analogies? In our view we already have an answer. The most successful teaching condition, in the large-scale study which we described in the last section, involved explicit training in analogies. Remember that the children were shown with the plastic letters how a change in the first letter of a word such as 'hen' transormed it into another word like 'pen' which rhymed. Here is an explicit experience with the kind of analogy which Usha Goswami showed to be so prevalent in young children generally but which we think might escape backward readers. The plastic letter method should not only have the general effect that it does on children's reading. It should also be particularly good at making children better at making analogies.

## The difficulties which backward readers have with sounds when they read

We have shown that backward readers tend to find it difficult to disentangle the sounds in words, and we have shown too that this difficulty must play a role in causing their problems with reading. But there is one link between these two skills – breaking words up into sounds and reading – which we have not yet talked about. It should be possible to demonstrate that many of the actual mistakes backward readers make when they read are due directly to their problem with sounds. Until this is shown, we shall not be able to say with complete certainty that there is a direct link between the problem and the way that these children read, or fail to read. The link certainly seems likely enough, because of the difficulties the problem ought to cause with the alphabetic code. But to convert this probability into a certainty we must look at the kind of mistakes backward readers tend to make *when they actually try to read*. Are these the result of an insensitivity to sounds?

How does one know if a child's mistake is a phonological one when he reads a word wrongly? After all, we have seen that in principle there are several different ways to read a word. Adding up sound segments ('c' + 'a' + 't' to reach 'cat') is of course one, and this is precisely what we should now expect backward readers to be rather bad at. But it is also quite possible that children read at least some words either as familiar sequences of letters or as familiar shapes: in both these cases breaking words up into their constituent sounds plays very little part. They could be muddled about the sequence of letters in the word or its shape.

Many people have claimed that children in general and young children in particular do rely very heavily on letter–sound correspondences and thus on their knowledge of speech sounds when they read. But in general the information behind such claims has been rather indirect. It has tended to come from studies which show that the sharper the child's awareness of sounds, the better he is at reading. That is certainly interesting but it does not definitely mean that children build up words by adding together segments of sound. We need a proper experiment to show this, and the nearest we come to it is a study by Estelle Doctor and Max Coltheart in London.

They had the simple idea of seeing whether children could be tricked by sentences like 'The sky is bloo' or 'She will soe a dress'. In terms of English spelling these sentences are not at all correct, but they sound all right. If one simply adds up the sounds typical of the letters in 'bloo' and 'soe' one hears the words 'blue' and 'sew'. So, these two experimenters argued, if children do read by sound they should find it harder to work out that there is something wrong with these sentences than with other sentences which sound wrong, like 'The sky is noe' or 'She will throo a dress'. They gave these two types of sentences (and others) to children of 6, 7, 8, 9, and 10 years, and found what they expected, at any rate with the younger children. The 6-, 7- and 8-year-olds had far more difficulty seeing that something was wrong with the sentences that sound correct than they did with the sentences which did not. This certainly does suggest that the children were reading 'phonologically' but one has to be cautious here. Introducing a written word that does not actually exist and must therefore be totally unfamiliar to the child could provoke her to read that word letter by letter in a way that is quite unusual. So we might have to retreat to the position that only in some circumstances – such as meeting a totally new word – do young children read 'phonologically'. That is the very least that this ingenious experiment suggests.

But if children who read normally for their age do take advantage of letter–sound correspondences when they are reading, what about backward readers who may very well have difficulty with the whole alphabetic system? Obviously they make many errors when they read, but once again we have to ask whether these are the result of a difficulty with isolating speech sounds. We must turn again to experiments.

These are to be found in the ingenious work of some psychologists in London. Uta Frith and Maggie Snowling set out to compare the mistakes made by a group of backward readers with those of another group of children with no reading problems.[5] Quite rightly these experimenters made sure that the two groups had reached the same reading level (8-10 years), which meant that the backward readers were considerably older than the others (10-12 years old as opposed to 8-10 years old).

The experimenters simply gave the children words to read. This apparently straightforward measure immediately raises some absorbing questions. The two groups should, overall, read as well as each other; after all they have reached the same reading levels. But if, as we are now suggesting, the groups have got to this same level of reading in different ways, they might make different types of mistakes. Backward readers ought to find any word which requires attention to its constituent sounds particularly difficult. One such word is what is often called a 'nonsense word' or even a 'non-word' (for example, 'molsmit' and 'slosbon' are nonsense words). Such words probably have to be read 'phonologically'.[6] One works out what they sound like by adding up the sounds associated with the letters. If backward readers find it difficult to see the relation between segments of sound and words, these nonsense words should be particularly hard for them to read.

The meaningful words which Frith and Snowling gave the children were of two kinds. One group were 'regular': their meaning could easily be worked out by their individual letters, 'Coffee' is an example of a word in Frith and Snowling's regular list. Reading it letter by letter naturally leads to the word 'coffee'. Of course, one cannot be sure that people do read a word like this by adding up the sounds associated with its letters, but the point of having this group of words becomes clearer when one considers the other words. These were 'irregular' words: they could not be read on a letter-by-letter basis. A word like 'laugh' is an irregular word, and was in fact included in the irregular list in this experiment. Reading it letter by letter and trying to add together the sounds associated with each letter leads one to something which is nowhere near the word 'laugh'.

The point of asking children to read both regular and irregular words is that one type of words can be deciphered by the sounds associated with their individual letters while the other cannot. If children do use letter–sound correspondences when they read, they should find the regular words easier than the irregular ones. So giving children both regular and irregular words to read and comparing the relative difficulty of the two kinds of word is another way of measuring children's use of speech sounds when they read. We must expect a smaller difference between regular and irregular words in backward readers than in other children.

Let us look first at the difference between meaningful and nonsense words. What happened was exactly what you would expect if backward readers do have difficulty with sound segments. They read the meaningful words as well as the other children, but were far worse with the nonsense words. The backward readers found it hard to decipher these and much harder than the other children did.

The comparison between regular and irregular words led to the same conclusion. Both groups of children found the regular words easier than the irregular ones, but this advantage of regular over irregular words was smaller among the backward readers than among other children. The second result, one should add, seems to be a fairly general one, since it happened in a Canadian study as well. Rod Barron, who works in Canada, also found that the advantage of regular over irregular words was more pronounced in children who read normally for their age than it was in backward readers. Here too backward readers seemed less willing, and were probably less able, to take advantage of the alphabetic code.

This conclusion is bolstered by a study by Maggie Snowling. She compared backward readers with younger children, making sure that the actual reading levels were the same (the correct reading-age design). Again she used nonsense words, but this time in a slightly different way. She presented two nonsense words at a time, and asked the child whether they were the same or not: sometimes they were identical, sometimes not. She either said the words or showed them, so that in effect one of her tasks was a reading task. She showed the child one word, said another and asked the child if they were the same. There were also other tasks which did not involve any reading. In one, the experimenter simply said both words, while in another she showed them both words.

It was the first of the two tasks which differentiated between the poor and the normal readers. The former found it particularly difficult and yet managed well when the experimenter showed them both the words or spoke them both. Once again the backward readers were poor at reading nonsense words – which depends on using speech segments – but this time we know that their difficulties were not with nonsense words *per se*, for they were at no disadvantages in the other tasks in which they did not have to read the words.

It seems fair to conclude that backward readers are less able than other children – even other children who read no better than they do – to take advantage of letter–sound correspondences. This is to be expected in children who are particularly poor at breaking words up into their component sounds. So we have an answer to our questions about the link between the backward readers' problem with sounds and the way that they read. Backward readers are bad at dealing with the sounds embedded in speech and this weakness also shows in the kind of mistakes that they make in reading. We have made a direct link with reading.

It is a tidy story. There is, we can now argue, a continuum going from children who are rather insensitive to the sounds in words through to those who are extremely good at spotting these sounds. This continuum plays an important role in deciding whether children read as well as expected or better or worse. Backward readers are part of this continuum, but the wrong part. That is one of the reasons, though almost certainly not the only reason, why many of them fail to learn to read. We can take comfort in the fact that our research and that of other people too shows that children can be moved up this particular continuum.

## Notes

1 This was described in the paper by Lundberg, Oloffson and Wall (1981).
2 This is the study, mentioned fleetingly in the last chapter, which was described in our 1983 *Nature* paper and in more detail in our 1985 monograph, *Rhyme and Reason in Reading and Spelling*.
3 We refer here to the training part of the same project.
4 Lynette Bradley's little book, *Assessing Reading Difficulties* (1984), and her paper in the *British Journal of Special Education* (1981) give details of the way that this training method can be used in remedial education.
5 This interesting study included as well a group of autistic children. However we shall limit our description of the results to the backward and normal readers.

6 One cannot be completely sure about this. It is in principle possible for people to read nonsense words on the basis of analogies with the letter sequences to be found in other words. This may still be 'phonological', but it is a far cry from converting each letter into a sound. Tony Marcel (1980) has made this point.

# 5

# Does the way backward readers read and spell reflect the way they think?

## The question of context

Some of the things that we have been saying go against the tide of current thinking about learning to read. A great deal of this thinking concentrates on the way children read whole passages of prose, and use parts of each passage to help work out what other parts mean. We, on the other hand, have concentrated on reading words rather than sentences. Most of our arguments have been about the reasons why backward readers find it difficult to read single words. Take, as an example, their apparent insensitivity to the sounds in words. A difficulty of this sort will hamper a child as much when she is trying to read single words as when she has to cope with whole sentences or even with longer passages of text. She will be in difficulty whether she is trying to read meaningful passages or not. So the problem works, so to speak, at the level of the single word. We have emphasized difficulties at this level because we think that it is here that the bulk of the typical backward reader's problems lie.

However, in recent years many psychologists, and teachers too, have made the reasonable claim that children pay close attention to the meaning of the passage which they are reading, and do their best to use its context to help them decipher what the words mean. Obviously we should respect this claim and try to find out exactly how children do use context while they read. It would be fruitless and sterile to ignore the fact that when a child reads she is doing a great deal more than just deciphering individual words.

We must ask another question as well. We need to know whether any of the backward readers' difficulties have anything to do with their use of context. And it is as well to note straightaway that there are two separate questions. Although it is probably true that the typical child's sensitivity to context plays a great part in her reading, this does not mean that the backward readers' problems must be traced back to some insensitivity to context. They may be as adept at using context as the next child.

Let us look first at psychologists' views on this question, and then at those of the world of education. Psychologists have a habit of dabbling in phrases whose inelegance outweighs their scientific value. The use of terms 'bottom up processes' and 'top down processes' is a case in point. This distinction between two kinds of reading has some merit and deserves attention: but the terms themselves are clumsy. We shall say what they mean and use them no more.

Both are about possible ways of reading passages of text. The first of the two terms refers to the kind of influences we have been discussing up to now. Our discussion has concentrated on the cues which words offer to people who are trying to decipher them. These cues – phonological, visual or orthographic – are to be found in the word itself. They are perceived and work their way up, so to speak, through the perceptual system to the appropriate part of the brain which then interprets this perceptual information. Everything starts at the 'bottom' with the cues offered by the word and then filters through to the brain which is the 'top'.

The alternative, the second of two possible ways, it to generate hypotheses – presumably with the help of the 'top' part of the system, the brain – and then to use these hypotheses to help work out what individual words or even whole phrases mean. Here the running is not made by the nature of the words' distinctive cues: the important thing is the child's use of inferences and hypotheses to help him decipher the text in front of him. It is a more active way of reading and it raises an obviously important question. To what extent do young children use what they already know or guess about the context to infer what particular words and phrases mean? Think now about backward readers and you face another question. Can they make as effective inferences as other children do when they read, and indeed can any of their problems be attributed to a difficulty in using the context to make inferences about the texts they are reading?

Psychologists have posed these questions often enough and so have educationalists like Frank Smith and Kenneth Goodman. Both are enthusiastic supporters of the idea that context plays a significant role, and of the importance of encouraging children to use it to make the kind of inferences just mentioned. Such is the strength of Goodman's feelings on this matter that he treats as anathema the kind of influence which we have been discussing in the previous chapter. For him the phonological, visual and orthographic cues are, on their own at any rate, relatively unimportant, and any attempt to help children by bumping up, say, their sensitivity to phonological cues is doomed to failure. He argues that children must be encouraged to use context and to form hypotheses while they read: 'All the central questions involved in reading are psycholinguistic ones, because reading is a process in which language interacts with thought.' Goodman is definitely not, to use the phrase for the last time, a 'bottom up' man.

The evidence which he offers for his 'interactive' thesis is based mainly on a detailed analysis of the kinds of mistakes – Goodman calls them 'miscues' – which children make when they read. There is no doubt that 'miscue analysis' has been a great step forward in the study of reading. Miscue analyses showed, for example, that very few of the things children get wrong when they read can be attributed simply to visual or phonological confusions. A child who reads 'little Miss Muffett sat on a chair' is doing more than just making a mistake. She is enlisting the context and also her considerable knowledge of the world to help her read.

We must take his point that children and adults use much more than just the visual, phonological and orthographic cues when they read. But where does this leave backward readers? Must we also conclude that these are sources of particular difficulty to children who are slow to learn to read? Of course it does not follow: and yet a lot of what Goodman writes suggests that it should. So keen is he on the importance of children using their knowledge of the world and of their language when reading that he argues that this quality is the epitome of skilled reading and something likely to be in short supply among backward readers.

Once again we face a causal question. In fact it boils down to two quite separate questions. The first is whether backwad readers have the idea of using the text's meaning to make inferences which will help them to read particular words and phrases properly, and also whether they depend on these inferences as much as other children do. If Goodman is right the answer to this first question is a definite 'No'. According to him one of the principal problems of the beginning reader is that he does not understand how context can help him, and so does not bother to make the inferences which are such an advantage to other children. The second question is about their ability to make this sort of inference. However much or however little backward readers depend on such inferences, we still have to discover how well they make them. It may be that backward readers depend on them and try to make them as much as other children, but that the inferences they come up with are not very good ones. This does not seem to be Goodman's idea but it is a possibility well worth investigating.

The answer to the first question seems to us to be beyond doubt. It is one of the few clear triumphs for the traditional kind of experiment (the mental-age match) which compares children of the same age and intelligence, but that is because the evidence is negative. That was the conclusion of an experiment run by Charles Perfetti, Susan Goldman and Thomas Hogaboam in Pittsburgh. They looked at a group of ten-year-old children, some of whom read well for their age, while the others were not so skilled, and they gave these children three tasks each made up of 20 words. In one (called 'isolation') they were shown the words one at a time, and were simply asked to read them. In another task ('list') they heard someone intoning a list of quite unrelated words before having to read each of the 20 words. Neither of these two tasks gave the children any helpful context.

However, the third task (the 'story') did. The child listened to someone reading out a story, and at 20 points in the narration she was shown (and was asked to read) the word which was the next to come in the story. So here the child had help from the context. What had gone before could help her read the word in front of her. The question was whether that added help would affect the backward readers as much as other children.

It did. Indeed it helped the backward readers even more than the others. The backward readers found it particularly difficult to read words in isolation or in the 'list' condition, but did much better in the story task. The other children also read better in that task but in their case the improvement was considerably smaller.

Here, then, is strong evidence that backward readers do depend on context. They use it to help them to work out the meaning of particular words and phrases, and they do so at least as much as other children and probably more so. These results go flat against the hypotheses of Goodman. So does the outcome of another study by the same Pittsburgh group. This time they looked not just at the effects of a helpful context, but also at one that was distinctly unhelpful. They wanted to know how well backward readers could cope with a word like 'dump' when the sentence which preceded it was 'Phil couldn't decide whether to go to the movies or to the party. Both sounded like lots of fun, but he finally decided to go to the dump'. The text which goes before the final word is designed to make the child expect either the word 'movies' or 'party' but instead he has to read 'dump'.

The experimenters looked at how long children took to read the target words when they were preceded by *unhelpful text* as

in the above example given, by *helpful text* ('The garbage men
. . . would have to drop off a load at the garbage dump'), and
by text designed neither to help nor to hinder. This
experiment confirmed the marked dependence of the backward readers on context. They were helped (again to a larger
extent than other children) by the helpful context, and they
were hindered to a far greater degree by the unhelpful text.
The conclusion seems clear. The backward readers did use
context and depended on it at least as much and probably
more than the normal run of children.

All this means that backward readers do know that context
is important and can help them work out the meaning of
various words and phrases. What about the second question?
Are backward readers as good as other children at using
context when context is all they have to go on? This was the
question asked in a well-known study by John Guthrie, an
American. His experiment is remarkable because it is one of
the very few which have made a claim for a deficit on the basis
of solid evidence. He compared backward readers of ten years
not only to children of the same age and intelligence (the usual
mental-age match), but also to normal children of seven years
whose reading levels were the same as those of the backward
readers (the more informative reading-age match). Guthrie
used a task which is often described as a maze test. The
children had choices to make at several points in a passage of
prose. He gave them sentences such as: 'The horses/flower/
talk lifted their ears. They had/were/some heard the forest
ranger's blanket/kept/voice. They are ready to go on/before a
trip/turned.' The children had to work out which, in each
instance of three linked words, was the right word for the
sentence.

The task caused considerable difficulty to the backward
readers and they managed to make more mistakes in it even
than the other children whose reading levels were the same as
their own. Here, then, is evidence for something that looks like
a deficit. Even when reading levels are controlled, backward
readers are particularly bad at working out what the next
word is if they have to rely entirely on the context to do so.

They may be at least as dependent as other children on context, and yet at the same time not so good at using it effectively when they have to.

Is this a serious deficit? There are, we think, a number of questions to be answered before we can be sure. One is whether the difficulty which Guthrie seems to have isolated would be as great when the child hears the sentences. In Guthrie's experiments everything was written down, and so we have no idea whether backward readers would be in difficulty with all types of context, or whether their problems are confined to written text. We suspect the latter.

Attempts to answer this have floundered for reasons which concern another question: i.e. how general is the difficulty which Guthrie found? Our colleague Ita Raz compared backward readers and normal readers of the same reading levels both in a written and spoken version of Guthrie's task.[1] To her surprise she found that backward readers fared as well as the others in the written version of her task, and in fact did rather better than the others in the task in which the sentences were spoken. Inconsistencies like this abound in experimental psychology. We cannot say yet whether the difference between Guthrie's results and Raz's mean that American and British backward readers differ or whether his experiment (or perhaps Ita Raz's) by an unfortunate chance produced results which do not represent the truth about the general run of backward readers.

## Thinking and reading

We have been talking about thinking, and in some ways we have plunged in feet first by looking at studies of reading straightaway. It is time that we took a step back and considered first what is known about children's thinking. Let us start with the most significant recent development in the study of children's growing intelligence. We know now that many of the intellectual skills which were said to be quite out of the question for young children – said, in fact, to represent 'deficits' – are perfectly possible for them. Their problem often has nothing to do with the possession of a skill (they do possess it) but with knowing when to apply it.

The evidence for this very general statement is still highly controversial, but to us it looks convincing. Here are some examples. It has been said that young children – children up to the age of roughly eight years – are unable to measure and indeed that they have no idea at all of the principles behind measurement. The evidence for this suggested deficit came from experiments by Piaget and his colleague Barbel Inhelder and Alina Szeminska, in which young children had to compare the height of two towers of bricks, one of which was built on a low table and the other on a much higher one. The children had various measures (a stick and some strips of paper) at their disposal, and Piaget was particularly interested in their use of these measures. He and his colleages found that the younger children hardly ever measured the two towers. Their favourite form of comparison was visual: they simply looked from tower to tower. The older children on the other hand evidently spotted how inaccurate this strategy was and resorted instead to measuring both towers with the stick or sometimes with strips of paper. The experimenters concluded that the principle of measurement is something which 'develops' in childhood and that it is quite absent in young children – a typical 'deficit' hypothesis about children's development.[2]

But it now seems that quite young children are able in principle to use a stick as an intervening measure to compare the length of two things. We showed this when we asked children to compare the depth of two holes sunk in two separate blocks of wood.[3] The important feature of this task was that the children could not see the full length of the two holes (nobody could) and so a direct visual comparison between the two was quite out of the question. In this experiment even children as young as five years managed to measure fairly consistently, and they seemed to know exactly what they were doing, as their answers were usually correct.

Why did they succeed in our task but fail in Piaget's? The answer can have nothing to do with any difference between experimenters, for when we gave the same five-year-olds Piaget's task they failed with us as miserably as Piaget's children had with him. To us there seems only one reasonable explanation. In Piaget's task the children did not appreciate how unreliable a direct visual comparison between the two towers would be, for otherwise they would have measured it. In our task a direct visual comparison was not possible, and therefore the children resorted to measurement.

Here, then, is an example of children actually possessing the ability to make a particular intellectual move, and yet not always doing so when they should. We are beginning now to talk not about deficits but about the way in which children learn to deploy their already considerable abilities on the appropriate occasions. Lest it seem that the example which we have given is one isolated instance, we should turn next to the recent argument about Piaget's famous conservation experiment. (Piaget and Szeminska, 1952).[4]

This is an experimental task which comes in two stages: in the first the child is shown two identical quantities which also appear identical – say, two rows of counters lined up alongside each other – and is asked to compare them. Usually he judges them to be equal, and then the second stage of the experiment begins. The experimenter changes the appearance of one of the rows, either by spreading it out or by bunching it up. Now the two rows, though equal in numbers, are unequal in length. Once again the child is asked to compare them, but this time often judges them, quite wrongly, to be unequal, usually saying that the longer row is also the more numerous. Younger children (children up to the age of about seven) tend to make this sort of judgement, whereas children older than that generally answer correctly.

Piaget's conclusion, and the conclusion of many others as well, is that the concept of invariance 'develops'. Younger children, he claims, must think that lengthening a row makes it more numerous and shortening it less so; older children understand that quantities do not change unless something is added or taken away. The hypothesis would be convincing, but for one awkward fact. Children who fail Piaget's version of the task often succeed in other versions which seem to make exactly the same demands on their understanding of the invariance principle.

The most famous example is the experiment by James McGarrigle and Margaret Donaldson from Edinburgh. Their new version of the task differed from Piaget's in one way only. Instead of shortening or lengthening the row themselves, they arranged matters so that the change was made, as though by accident, by a marauding 'naughty' teddy bear. Otherwise the task was the same as Piaget's. But the results were very different. A sizeable number of children even as young as four years managed to produce the correct answer in the teddy bear version of the task: and it is worth noting that many of these same children failed badly when they were given Piaget's version of the task. The reason for this striking difference between two versions which at first sight seem to have the same essential structure and to differ from each other in one apparently trivial detail only, is still a matter of some controversy. However, the children's success in the one task and their failure in the other does suggest once again that they have the ability to solve problems such as these, but do not always use it to full effect. We are faced not with an intellectual blank in young children, but with an initial difficulty on their part in taking advantage of abilites which they certainly do possess.[5]

All this may seem a long way from learning to read and spell, but there is a striking similarity between the way children tackle cognitive problems and what they must learn about reading and spelling. In both they have to choose which strategy is the right one and they must learn that different strategies work better with different circumstances. In cognitive problems it is sometimes quite all right to make a direct visual comparison when one wants to know about the relative height of two different things, but at other times such comparisons are distinctly risky, and it is best to resort to measurement. Reading and spelling are much the same.

They, too, involve a range of strategies, as we have seen. Phonological, visual, orthographic, contextual – all these are different ways of reading, and all of them are needed at different times. For example, phonological strategies will not be much use to us when we are trying to read or write words which are highly irregular. And visual familiarity is no help at all to someone who encounters an unfamiliar word the like of which he has never seen before.

Thus it seems quite possible that a child might get things wrong in reading or writing simply because he fails to use the right skill at the right time. There are times when he could, say, decipher a written word by latching on to its letter – sound correspondences in that word – something he is in principle able to do – but he does not. This is all speculation of course. It is one possibility, whereas the deficit hypothesis is another. The important thing is to realize how different the two approaches are. One of them grants the child the basic skills and argues that improvement in reading and spelling comes through learning how to apply these skills in the right way at the right time: the other presumes that the child gets better at reading and writing because he acquires new skills.

The fact is that the same question can be asked about the poor reader. Are his problems due to some specific deficit as everyone seems to have assumed? Or can one argue that he does not suffer from a deficit at all, and that he has all the skills needed to learn to read and spell but does not take full advantage of these skills? We shall take this second possibility very seriously in the rest of this chapter.

## The differences between reading and spelling

Let us return to the point about the question of strategies and to the idea that children may use a particular skill to help them in one task, but not in another. Does this apply to written language? We must begin to answer this question by considering what different tasks there are. In fact the simplest and yet the most significant distinction is between reading and spelling. Here are two different accomplishments which children acquire at roughly the same time, but do they learn them in the same way?

You may ask if there is any reason for thinking that they should not. After all, both reading and writing apparently use the same alphabetic code. True, children often fail to spell words properly even though they can read them with ease. So do adults. This discrepancy between reading and spelling may be due simply to the fact that spelling is a matter of producing words, and reading of recognizing them. On the whole producing any kind of language is harder than understanding it, as any one learning a foreign language will ruefully admit. So there seem to be no *a priori* grounds for thinking that the two tasks are learned any differently, and fairly good common sense reasons for believing that the child must tackle both in much the same way. This common sense belief must have been quite widely held because psychologists virtually ignored the question of spelling for many years and concentrated instead on the way children learn to read. They assumed that anything they found out about children's reading would apply equally well to their spelling.[6] But now we have a fair amount of evidence to show that this assumption is quite wrong.

Our evidence starts with a simple but surprising observation. It is that young children often spell words correctly but cannot read them. They cannot read them even if, after a suitable interval, they are shown these words correctly spelled in their own handwriting. The discovery is important because it demonstrates a surprising degree of separation between the way they spell and the way they read. There is a two-way discrepancy. Children read some words which they cannot spell and also (the surprising pattern) spell other words without being able to read them. They must, therefore, be setting about the two activities in different ways.

The experiment which demonstrated this two-way discrepancy was exceedingly simple:[7] We saw children whose ages ranged from 6½ to 7¾ years and gave them the same list of 30 words to read on some occasions and to spell on others. The words were fairly common ones and included some, like 'mat', which were highly regular and which could be read and spelled solely on the basis of letter – sound correspondences, and others, like 'people', which could not.

Then we looked at each child's records to see how well he read and spelled each word. If you take each word separately it is easy to see that there are only four possibilities: (1) that the child could both read and spell the word in question, (2) that he could neither read nor spell it properly, (3) that he could read the word but not spell it, and finally – the interesting possibility – (4) that he could spell it correctly and yet could not read it. The first important thing to note about our results is that the younger children – those whose ages were below seven years – did in fact spell some words which they could not read. Not so the older children. In their case the words fell into the first three categories and there were very few instances of words spelled correctly but not read. So the older children could read all the words that they could spell. The young children could not. We take this to mean that the younger ones set about the two activities, reading and spelling, in different ways. The two-way discrepancy (some words read, but not spelled and others spelled but not read) seems to prove this. So now we must consider what these different ways are.

The kinds of words which fell into the two discrepant categories most persistently give us a strong clue. Let us look first at the words which children most often managed to read but failed to spell. The four words which fell into this category most frequently were definitely not of the type which can easily be spelled or read on a letter by letter basis. They were 'school', 'light', 'people' and 'egg', and it is easy to see that these are not regular words. In contrast, the other discrepant words were phonetically regular: the four words which were most often spelled correctly but not read were 'bun', 'leg', 'mat' and 'pat'.

This suggests the simple hypothesis that at this age children spell phonologically. For them writing a word is predominantly a matter of alphabetic letters and phonological segments. They adopt the phonological code. But it is quite a different matter when they read. This they do in chunks. Either they recognize familiar words – 'school' is an example of a word which they will see many times a day – or they perceive familiar sequences of letters as sequences without having to work out what sound is symbolized by each letter. The simple explanation for children adopting these strategies is that it is the natural thing for a young child. Let us take reading first. When a child first begins to recognize and to decipher words he has already had several years' experience of distinguishing and recognizing visual patterns: he is very good at it, and it is not at all surprising that he manages to do it again when he begins to attend to familiar words. Many of these – 'school', 'stop' and 'police' for example – he will see over and over again. Why should he not recognize these as he recognizes, say, a bus or a familiar trademark? Nothing could be more natural.

But spelling would be quite another matter. Although young children are good at recognizing patterns, on the whole they are rather poor at reproducing them. At the ages which we are discussing children's drawings, although lively, are not accurate. Though a child may recognize a word as a whole he will have considerable difficulty in producing this whole on paper. When he writes he will not take to the visual strategy naturally. What is he left with? Obviously there is the phonological strategy, but it is not just a matter of adopting that *faute de mieux*. It is also the natural thing to do. When you spell you start with the spoken word; the act of speaking a word provides a cue which could help with the phonological segments. When anyone speaks he moves his vocal apparatus in a series of movements, which are known as articulatory movements. These roughly correspond with the phonological segments in the word. Speaking the word might help the child to work out what its constituent sounds are. That may be why children adopt the phonological strategy when they write but not when they read.

The hypothesis is plausible enough, and further evidence for it comes from the second part of the experiment, when we went on to a more complex manouevre. According to our ideas, children should begin to read those odd words which they had not read but had managed to spell properly if we were to encourage them to read on a letter–sound basis. Our argument was that children must be able to construct these particular words phonologically because they spell them. Thus if they also read phonologically they should cope with these words very well. We therefore turned to nonsense words. We gave the children a list of these words to read and asked them to read each word on a letter by letter basis, which they seemed to do after some persuasion. But without the children realizing it the list contained more than just nonsense words. In it we embedded real words and in fact with each child we inserted all the words which he had not been able to read before. Some of these, of course, had fallen into the interesting category of words which the child had spelled but not read.

In these new circumstances the children now began to read these last words very well. The encouragement to read phonologically helped them to read words which earlier they had spelled but not read: it had no appreciable effect on the words which they had neither read nor spelled previously. It seems that young children can be sure of reading words which they can spell when they are encouraged to read phonologically. Here indeed is strong evidence for the idea that they spell but often do not read phonologically.

But there is other evidence as well. Two well-known studies separately suggest that children take naturally to the phonological strategy when they write but not when they read. One, which deals with writing, is a study by Charles Read.[8] He became interested in a group of nursery school-children – the nursery was at Harvard – who could not read yet but who did seem to know about letters and sounds: they had learned which sounds typically go with which individual alphabetic letters. Read's most important observation was that these children often wrote words the spelling of which at first sight looked chaotic but which actually preserved the rules of correspondence between letters and sounds in a rather ingenious way; for example, 'halpt' for 'helped' or 'Fes sowemeg in woodr' for 'fish swimming in water' are by no means bad shots at representing the words' sounds in a letter by letter way.

But do children do the same thing when they actually begin to read? Our answer, or at any rate our hypothesis's answer, is a definite 'no', and it receives some strong support from a second well-known study, which took place in Canada. Rod Barron and Jon Baron (no relation, just orthographic neighbours) adopted a technique known as 'concurrent vocalization', which involves the child repeating a word over and over again while doing another task. The purpose is to impede the phonological strategy, and experimenters use it to find out whether children need this strategy in particular tasks. A task which depends on some phonological analysis should be more difficult to do if at the same time one is intoning a word all the time than if one does it silently.

This argument is controversial and one certainly has to be cautious about drawing any firm conclusions from studies which use the technique, but it it is nevertheless an ingenious way of looking at the role of the phonological strategy in reading and spelling. Barron and Baron gave the children various tasks in which they were shown a series of pictures: a word was written besides each picture and the child had to check whether the word was appropriate in some way to the picture next to it. In one task (the Rhyme task) she had to mark off those pairs in which the word rhymed with the name of the picture next to it (a picture of a horn for example by the word 'corn'). This task plainly involves attention to phonological segments. Whether the other main task, which was a reading task, also demanded a phonolgical strategy was the principal question posed by this experiment. Here the child simply had to decide whether the word 'meant' the same as the picture (sometimes it did, sometimes not): so this was a reading task and of course the experimenters' purpose was to find out whether the children depended on the phonological strategy here as well.

Their test was to give the children both kinds of task in two ways. In one, the children had to intone the word 'double' without a pause right through the task. In the other condition they worked silently. The results were simple and striking. Concurrent vocalization did make the Rhyme task more difficult, and thus did seem to have a considerable effect on the children's attention to phonological segmentation. But it did not affect the reading task. Even children as young as six years read words as successfully when they were intoning the 'double double' chant as when they were not.

These results, which surprised the experimenters as much as many other people, suggest that young children's phonological strategies may be less important in young children's reading than in other more directly phonological tasks. The study certainly gives indirect support to our hypothesis of a separation between learning to read and learning to spell. It also suggests another way of examining the idea.

The same interference which has no effect on children's reading could hinder their spelling quite considerably. If concurrent vocalization does get in the way of phonological segmentation it should make spelling much harder. It does. Yuko Kimura, working in Oxford and Osaka in Japan, showed this in a study of English and Japanese children. The English children were given 10 pictures and had to write down the names of the objects in all of them – a spelling task – on two different occasions. On one occasion they wrote the words while intoning the chant 'Bla, bla', whereas on the other they wrote and were silent. Here concurrent vocalization had an effect. It was considerably harder for the children to spell the words properly when they had intone 'bla, bla' than when they wrote in silence.[9] This suggests that the phonological strategy does play an important part in spelling, but one has to be cautious because writing involves much more than just spelling. The child also has to make the correct arm and hand movements when writing: saying a word repeatedly might get in the way of that. How does one control for this?

This is where the Japanese children are important. Remember that there are two kinds of Japanese script. One (*kanji*) consists of logographs and makes no phonological demands at all: the other (*kana*) does because each symbol signifies a syllable. If the effect of concurrent vocalization on writing is a phonological one, as we suspect, then it should have no impact on writing *kanji* but should hold back writing *kana*. But if it is just a matter of concurrent vocalization getting in the way of writing movements in general, then it should hamper *kana* and *kanji* alike. The first of these alternatives turned out to be the right one. Yuko Kimura found an effect but only with *kana*. The Japanese children wrote *kanji* as well when they intoned words as when they did not.

Putting all this together we can conclude that there is now considerable support for our ideas about young children's reading and spelling. The children do specialize. They possess strategies, such as the phonological and perhaps the visual strategy, which they do use but use sparingly. They could in principle use the phonological strategy when they read and, as we have shown, they can be encouraged to do so. But often they do not. Their spelling seems as specialized, and here they do not take to using the 'chunking' strategies which come so easily to them when they read. This is why they manage to spell regular words yet fail with irregular ones.


## Children who spell badly but read well

All this is a far cry from any deficit. It is not the lack of a particular skill which concerns us now, but its deployment. Just as in the logical tasks which we discussed earlier, so it seems to be with reading and spelling. One of the child's main problems, we think, is how to use her skills to their full advantage. Now we must consider whether poor readers and spellers have the same problem as well, but in an exaggerated form.

There is some excellent evidence on this question in the deservedly influential work of Uta Frith. It is largely due to her that the distinction between children's reading and spelling is now recognized as important. Her work on the subject started with a group of children who read without any problem but whose spelling was appalling. Their frequent spelling mistakes, she found, tended to be 'phonetic', i.e. the spelling was wrong, but it did convey the sound of the words the children were trying to write. 'Coff' for 'cough', and 'surch' for 'search' are two of Frith's examples of phonetic spelling errors. The fact that they managed to represent the sounds of the words that they were trying to write *and still* make many spelling errors is deeply interesting. It suggests that they made mistakes because they concentrated on the letter–sound relationship and did not remember or use their memory for whole words or for sequences like '-ough'.

Uta Frith's next piece of evidence converted this idea into a virtual certainty. She asked these poor spellers to write down nonsense words, like 'zatest' and 'usterand', which she dictated to them. Now they began to spell efficiently. This must have been because they spelled these strange words by letter–sound correspondences and did so without any difficulty. All this seems to point to the conclusion that the poor spellers understand letter–sound correspondence very well, but cannot cope with 'chunks'. But so far the evidence has only been about these children's spelling.

Uta Frith now turned to these children's reading and to her surprise found virtually the mirror image of what she had seen in their spelling. One thing that she discovered was that the poor spellers found it much harder to read and interpret mispelled words like 'nite' which sound right but look wrong, than ones like 'nght' which look rather like the correct word but certainly sound wrong. It is as though the 'chunks' are very important to these children when they read, while the letter–sound relationships now sink into insignificance. They spell in one way and read in another.

Here is a clear case of a difficulty in deploying skills. The poor spellers use one strategy in spelling, another in reading. In fact their narrow specialization reminds us very strongly of the normal run of six-year-old children. Once again the problem does not seem to involve a deficit. None of the essential skills seem to be absent. The poor speller just employs them too narrowly.

So we have met our first example of a group of children who

are in considerable difficulty with learning about written language and yet do not seem to suffer from any deficit. But it may be a special case: after all these children were only poor at spelling. Can this analysis ever be applied to children who have difficulties with reading as well as with spelling? Or do their problems always have to be traced back to some deficit or other?

## Poor readers and the differences between reading and spelling

We must go back to the normal course of learning to read and spell and consider first what typically happens to children who are not beset by any difficulties with written language. Our research and Uta Frith's suggest that children's approach to reading and spelling changes very markedly during their first three years or so at school. From the start they adopt the right strategies, but in a narrow way. By the age of, or at any rate by the reading level of, around seven years, they become more flexible. The rigid separation between reading and spelling seems to disappear. No longer do we find the curious two-way discrepancy between these two activities, which must be a sign that children begin to see the connection between them and begin to treat them in much the same way. We can conclude that children start by reading in one way and spelling in another, but soon blur that unhelpful distinction.

Is this also true of poor readers? When they reach the reading level of seven or so years (by which time they will be considerably older than seven) do they also begin to use their skills more broadly? Our research suggests that they do not. Poor readers, we have found, persist in using one strategy for reading and quite another for spelling more stubbornly and for a longer time than other children *of the same reading and spelling levels.*

We found this in much the same kind of experiment as before but now with a large group of backward readers – 60 in all – and a comparable group of younger normal children. We gave these children the same words to read and also to spell. Once again the words were a mixture: some could be easily spelled and read on a letter-by-letter basis, others not. Once again we used the four categories: (1) words read and spelled correctly, (2) words neither read nor spelled, (3) words read but not spelled, and (4) words spelled correctly but not read.

Here too we found instances of the fourth curious category. Children in both groups spelled some words which they did not manage to read. Naturally there were other words which they read but did not spell. So we confirmed the existence of this odd two-way discrepancy in children at the beginning stages of learning to read and to write. But there was also a difference between the two groups. The two-way discrepancy was larger among the backward readers. A greater proportion of their mistakes fell into the two discrepant categories.

Surely this means that the degree of independence between reading and spelling is greater among the backward readers than among the other children. Although the two groups had actually reached the same level of reading and spelling, the backward readers were more specialized and less ready to take advantage of skills *which they actually possessed*. We know very well that what we have called the phonological strategy is not developed at all well in these children. But now we find that what phonological skills they do have remain quite firmly attached and restricted to spelling, and also that their chunking skills are largely used for reading.

Here is the first piece of firm evidence that the problems of these children cannot be completely written off as deficits. It now seems that they also have difficulties with the proper use of the skills that they do possess.[10] The point has great practical significance, for it means that we must do more than just try to teach such children new skills. We also have to show them how to organize their own capacities more effectively. Getting rid of a deficit and teaching children how to take advantage of their own considerable skills are two entirely different things.

Which should the teacher try to do and how should he set

about it? We shall return to these questions in our final two chapters.

## Notes

1 Ita Raz's experiment has not been published yet.
2 The experiment is described in chapter 2 of the book by Piaget, Inhelder and Szeminska (1960).
3 The experiment with the blocks of wood was done by Peter Bryant and Hanka Kopytynska (1976).
4 A description of the experiment is given in the book by Piaget and Szeminska (1952).
5 There is at least one other connection to be made between Piagetian theory and reading, and that is a far more positive one. It was made in a book by Ferreiro and Teberosky (1979) who looked at children's ideas about written language before they begin to read. The authors pursued the idea that children construct their own hypotheses about reading and writing. It is an ingenious and absorbing book.
6 This narrow view was torpedoed by the 1980 book on spelling which was ably put together by Uta Frith.
7 We described this work in our 1979 paper in *Developmental Medicine and Child Neurology*, and also in our chapter in Uta Frith's 1980 book.
8 This is the paper which Charles Read published in the *Harvard Educational Review* (1971).
9 We have confirmed the English side of these results several times. See our chapters in the books edited by Martlew (1983), and by Rutter (1983).
10 This point is made in more detail in the chapter by Peter Bryant in the book edited by Das, Mulcahy and Wall (1983).

# 6

# Dyslexia, dyslexias

We started this review of the evidence in the same way as the subject began a hundred years ago: with Hinshelwood's intuition about word blindness. As it happens, his particular idea that everything could all be traced back to some visual efficiency has turned out to be wrong and has been widely abandoned. However, his more general assumption that there is a group of people who read badly because of forces which have very little to do with the way the rest of the population read has had a profound effect. Yet much of the evidence that we have reviewed does not fit well with the idea of a separate and distinct group.

There is, however, one powerful reason for being cautious about assuming that the alternative – of the continuum – must be true. It is that poor children with reading difficulties are quite obviously different from each other. It may be that their difficulties vary too – that there are different kinds of reading difficulties. Why should this mean discontinuity? In fact on its own it does not. Even if there are different types of backward reader there may also be the same different types of normal reader. In other words there may be several continua.

But we must still be careful. The experiments discussed in chapters 4 – 5 could have failed to demonstrate the existence of an idiosyncratic group because they ignored the possibility of differences among backward readers. All the experiments which we have described so far lump backward readers together in one group and then compare them to a group of normal children. To do that one must believe that the vast majority of backward readers suffer from the same deficit as each other. Otherwise the experiment will not work. If some, but only a few, of the backward readers suffer from the difficulty which you have in mind, then that particular difficulty will not show up clearly in your experiment. It will be swamped by the differences among the backward readers. Fortunately several people who have done research on children's reading difficulties have treated the possibility that these difficulties do take different forms in different children quite seriously. Broadly speaking the studies done by these people have taken one of two forms. Either they involve quite large numbers of backward readers, who are then divided up into several different 'subgroups', or they concentrate on one backward reader – as a distinct individual – only.

## Are there different types of reading difficulty?

Let us return for the moment to our discovery that backward readers are on the whole remarkably insensitive to rhyme and alliteration (as shown at the end of chapter 3). We found this insensitivity in most of the children but we also found a few who had no difficulty with our tasks whatsoever. These children are a minority, but it is a minority which demands an explanation.

Others have drawn attention to such differences and indeed it has often been claimed that there is no such thing as 'the' backward reader. Children with reading difficulties, the argument goes, are all different. They are a mixed group who set about the task of learning to read in different ways from one another. The claim is important and it could affect teaching methods. It might, for example, mean that it would be better to teach some backward readers in one way and others quite differently. How does one assess this claim?

There is one essential rule. It is that *differences among backward readers demonstrate specific types of reading difficulty only when these differences are something to do with the causes of the children's problems with reading*. It is no surprise at all that differences are to be found among groups of backward readers: indeed it would be very surprising if they were not different from each other. Any group of children – no matter how similar their backrounds – will throw up striking differences. These differences are only relevant if they are associated with the reasons behind the reading difficulties.

We can make the point with the help of a preposterous example. Suppose that we asked a group of backward readers to run 100 metres and found that some ran the course swiftly, while others were disappointingly slow. Then we could divide them into two groups – fast and slow running backward readers. It would be a genuine difference but it would be rash to go on to claim that the reading difficulties of the one group could be traced back to their great speed, and of the other group to their snail-like pace on the running track.

How does one establish that there are differences among backward readers which stem from the fact that their reading problems have different causes? How, in other words, does one show that there are different types of reading difficulty? There are several steps and, as we shall soon see, they have not yet all been taken. But the first and most obvious is to make sure that the same differences are not to be found among children who read normally for their age. You cannot claim that a particular type of behaviour which you find among some backward readers is responsible for holding their reading back if children who read normally behave in exactly the same way and can be divided up into identical groups. The simple precaution of checking whether the same differences are to be found in other children too would take care of our preposterous running example: children who read well would fall into fast and slow running groups in much the same way.

Then there is the question of who the comparable normal readers should be. By now the answer ought to be clear. They must be children whose reading level is identical to that of the backward readers in question. Once again we have to make a reading-age match. It would be absurd to do anything else. Suppose that one looked at the pattern of reading and spelling errors and found that one lot of backward readers made some characteristic mistakes and another lot some quite different mistakes. It would be quite wrong to compare them to a group of children of the same age who read normally and therefore much better than the backward readers. The ways in which children read and write do change as they get better at it. If one found a different pattern among a normal group of readers who had reached a higher level, that difference might merely be something to do with stages of reading and nothing at all to do with the actual reading problems of the backward readers.

This is an essential first step. Having taken it, one would need to go further and look at the effects of training. If there are different types of backward readers, each type with its different handicap, then removing this handicap through teaching should have a prodigious effect on their reading. What is more, different groups of backward readers should benefit from different types of instruction. Once again results of this sort would clinch the causal argument. These are obvious moves, but still a bit of a pipe dream because no one has ever managed to take the first step, let alone the second.

Let us look at some of the claims that there are different types of reading difficulties. One interesting point about them is that virtually everyone agrees that a substantial proportion of backward readers suffer from a difficulty with isolating the sounds in words and sentences. Of course each scheme also suggests that there is, as well, at least one other group which does not have this problem, and the commonest alternative candidate is a visual problem. An early and very well-known example of this is the research of Elena Boder who works in California. On the basis of her great experience with backward readers she argued that their difficulties can take more than one form. She decided that their errors fall into two major categories: 'dysphonetic', or 'dyseidetic'. The first kind of mistake is the result of insensitivity to the sounds in words, and the second of a difficulty with taking in and remembering the visual appearance of written words.

Boder also argued that these two types of mistakes tell different backward readers apart. Some tend to make one type of mistake predominantly, some the other. She claimed that there were three recognizable groups of backward readers: the *dysphonetic* group who tend to be very confused about the sounds of the words that they are trying to read and to spell; the *dyseidetic* group who seem to have a reasonable grasp of the sounds in words at any rate when they try to spell them, but cannot remember their appearance and thus have difficulties with irregular words which cannot be read phonetically; and the *mixed* group of backward readers, who make both kinds of error and thus seem to be afflicted by both kinds of difficulty.

Here are some more details of Boder's interesting scheme. A typical child in the dysphonetic group will read words 'globally' with little attention to the individual letters, and will be hard put to it to read any new words which are not in his sight vocabulary (not, that is, words which he recognizes immediately). His spelling is poor and full of gross phonetic errors, such as 'rember' for 'remember', 'refets' for 'rough' and 'mar' for 'marmalade'. 'He is', Boder claims, 'unable to analyse the auditory gestalt of the word into its component sounds and syllables: he is unable to syllabicate'. It is interesting to note that her actual description of children of this sort fits well with the general picture that we have been painting of the backward reader's difficulties. We too have pointed to their difficulty with the sounds of the words which they are trying to spell. But our emphasis is different from hers in some ways. She says of the dysphonetic child that 'because he cannot read phonetically, he cannot spell phonetically'. We argue that backward readers tend to rely on other strategies when they read, but use a phonetic one when they spell, albeit with very little success.

We should turn now to her claim for a dyseidetic group, for this from the point of view of much of what we have said in earlier chapters is more surprising. These are children whose main difficulty, according to Boder, is a visual one. They cannot remember the visual appearance of words and hence have great difficulty when reading and spelling words which cannot be constructed letter by letter and sound by sound. A dyseidetic child reads by ear. For example, he may not read 'laugh' at all or he may read it as 'log' or 'loge', and he may read 'business' as 'bussyness' or 'talk' as 'talc'. When the child spells, he does so phonetically and his mistakes are phonetic ones: 'laf' for 'laugh' and 'burd' for 'bird'. So Boder is making two striking claims. One is that there are backward readers who do not suffer any particular problem with the sounds of words, and the other that the main problem for these same children is a visual one.

There must be some justice in the first of these two claims. As we have noted, we ourselves did find some backward readers – a small minority – who had no difficulty at all with the task of detecting whether words rhymed or not. But the second claim for a visual problem is controversial since the experimental evidence given in chapter 3 does nothing to support the idea of visual difficulties. However this evidence came from studies which simply lumped all backward readers together in one group. It is still possible that the visual difficulties of a few might have been submerged in the flood of phonological mistakes of the majority of backward readers. We have to leave the suggestion open for the moment.

The children in Boder's third group are unfortunate enough to be afflicted by both kinds of difficulty. Her view of their future is not at all optimistic. At any rate she suggests that they will need most help.

She studied 107 children between the ages of 8 and 16 years (it is interesting to note that only 15 of them were girls), all of whom had fallen at least two years behind in their reading. She looked at the mistakes which they made when reading and spelling words, and decided that of the 107 children, 100 fell clearly into one of her three groups. The dysphonetic group accounted for 67 of these 100 children, the dyseidetic group only 10, and the mixed group 23. This categorization is important as the fact that there were so few in the most controversial category – backward readers competent with sounds but held back by a visual weakness – could mean that other people's failure to find visual problems among backward readers could be explained by the very small number of children with this sort of problem.

The study is sensitive and in many ways quite convincing, but we must now consider whether it passes the tests which we set at the beginning of this section, and the answer is that it does not. The most obvious gap, and the most serious one, is that she did not compare these backward readers to normal readers of the same reading level. Indeed as far as we know she did not compare them to normal children at all. So we have no guarantee that these different types are unique to backward readers, and indeed there is some evidence that they are not. Recently Jon Baron and Rebecca Treiman from Philadelphia have produced evidence that children in general can conveniently be divided into either 'Phoenician' or 'Chinese' groups. The 'Phoenicians' (so called because the Phoenicians invented scripts in which symbols signify sounds) tend to lean heavily on the correspondence between letters and sounds. The 'Chinese' on the other hand tend to rely on their visual memory for words and are called that because, according to Baron and Treiman, they treat English written words as logographs: they remember them as wholes.

This, too, is a controversial theory but we mention it to show that what Boder is claiming for backward readers may be true of other children as well. If that were so, then Boder would be telling us about ways of reading and writing which might have nothing to do with the reasons for the difficulties of backward readers. (In the next section of this chapter we shall be presenting evidence that the differences among backward readers are exactly the same as those that are to be found among other children with no reading problems.)

There are other schemes which are very similar to Boder's but they do not solve this particular problem. Recently John Mitterer in Canada claimed that he could divide a group of backward readers quite neatly into a 'whole word group' and a 'recoding group'. The former, like Boder's dysphonetic group, could recognize words by their visual appearance but had great difficulty disentangling the sounds in words. They were, for example, thrown badly off course when they had to read words in an unusual visual form – LiKe this. The second group on the other hand seemed, like Boder's dyseidetic group, to have no difficulty handling letter–sound correspondence but were at sea with the visual appearance of words. These children found it much easier to read and spell words which are regular – words, that is, which can be read or spelled in a letter-by-letter way.

Mitterer did at least compare his backward readers to children who read normally for their age. He found that this sort of difference was not nearly so sharp among normal children and so he concluded that he had found something peculiar to backward readers. But he compared the backward readers to the wrong children: he used the 'mental-age match'. All the children – backward readers and good readers alike – were about eight years old. This meant, of course, that the good readers had reached a higher level of reading than the backward readers. So it is entirely possible that the difference between the two groups could simply be a matter of the level of reading. At one level children – good or backward readers – might fall readily either into a 'whole word' or into a 'recoding group'; at a higher level children might no longer fit so neatly into these two categories. A developmental change of this sort is not so implausible. After all we saw in the last chapter how children tend to mix strategies as they grow older: this surely would diminish the kind of specialization endemic in the type-casting attempted by Boder, Baron and Treiman and Mitterer. We cannot say who is right yet, because the right kind of comparison has yet to be made.

There are other schemes for individual differences among backward readers. But none as far as we can see meets the reasonable standard that we have set them: having divided backward readers into various groups, none then compares them to normal children at the same reading level. Without this essential first step we simply cannot make the next move towards finding the right ways to teach different types of children in difficulty with reading.

We do not wish to deny the existence of differences among backward readers. In fact, we believe that there may well be different reasons why different backward readers fail as they do. But what these various reasons are still has to be established. When that happens we shall still have to face the question of the continuum. Boder's and Mitterer's studies, and most other attempts to divide backward readers into different types, admit the existence of a substantial group – often the majority – who have difficulty isolating and putting together sounds in words. Our own work has confirmed this sort of difficulty among backward readers and has demonstrated that it is part of a continuum stretching from unexpectedly poor to equally unexpectedly good readers. So, the children who have difficulty with sounds could be part of such a continuum, while the other types of backward reader are not. But there is even an alternative to this: these other types could be part of some other continuum. There may be other reasons and other forces which lead some children do better and others worse than expected at reading.

But we should not get bogged down with these fancies. These are questions to be thought about when the bread-and-butter issue of whether there really are genuine and distinctive patterns of reading difficulty is settled. We shall have to do better designed research to find that out.


## Single cases and the analogy between 'acquired' and 'developmental' dyslexia

We come now to the other major source of evidence about differences between backward readers, and that is the detailed study of individual cases. The people who are most insistent that backward readers are a separate and distinctive bunch of children are often the parents, remedial teachers or psychologists who have had a great deal of contact with individual backward readers. Detailed knowledge of individual children with reading difficulties frequently seems to convince people that they are an idiosyncratic group.

Why should this be so? One obvious reason is that you are bound to learn about a child's peculiarities when you know him well. It seems very likely that people who get to know individual backward readers are so struck by their peculiarities that they conclude that there must be something distinctive about these children. These assumptions may be right, and we do not in any way wish to belittle them. On the contrary we think that our understanding of the nature of children's reading problems would be a great deal poorer without the help of detailed investigations of individual cases. But we also think that such studies are unconvincing without the help of some basic precautions. These are usually neglected.

We shall concentrate on some recent attempts to make a connection between 'developmental' and 'acquired' dyslexia. They are in many ways the most convincing example of the use of single cases to justify the idea of dyslexia as a separate entity. 'Developmental' dyslexia is the term which is often used for the children whose problems we have been discussing throughout this book. 'Acquired dyslexia' on the other hand refers to people who originally had no problem about learning to read, but who later on, because of some kind of damage to their brain, either lost their ability to read or at least found it a great deal more difficult than before.[1]

Acquired dyslexics are thought of as a distinct group. They have something in common – damage to the brain – which other people do not have or at any rate not so severely. But the most interesting thing about them is that they are not a homogeneous group. It is quite clear that there are different forms of acquired dyslexia. One is known as 'deep dyslexia'. The unfortunate people who come under this heading seem to be virtually incapable of the kind of phonological analysis which we have discussed at length in earlier chapters. They cannot, for example, decipher nonsense words. They do read some real words, however, but often make an intriguing error which was noticed first by John Marshall and Freda Newcombe at Oxford. This takes the form of seeing one word, but reading it as another which has a similar meaning or comes from the same category as the correct word. 'Rose' for 'daffodil' and 'pixie' for 'gnome' are typical examples. Such mistakes seem to show that to some extent it is possible to read without analysing sounds in words. However this sort of reading seems to be prone to confusion.

Another similar though less drastic form of acquired dyslexia is called 'phonological dyslexia'. It also involves difficulties with the analysis of sounds but not such severe ones. The people who are called 'phonological dyslexics' have difficulty reading nonsense words, and they make mistakes which suggest that they are leaning heavily on the visual appearance of the word. These mistakes are called derivational errors ('weigh' read as 'weight') and visual errors ('camp' read as 'cape'). Phonological dyslexics seem to use the visual appearance of words and perhaps their orthographic sequences as well, rather than analysing them into phonological segments.

There is a third form of acquired dyslexia which is sharply different from the other two. This is 'surface dyslexia': the people called 'surface dyslexics' seem to have nothing wrong with their phonological skills. They can read and write nonsense words. Their difficulty is with words which one cannot read simply with the help of letter–sound correspondences. These people find it very difficult to remember and to read irregular words. Quite often they read these words phonologically and turn them into nonsense words by doing so. They might, for example, read 'broad' as 'brode'. Another difficulty is that they muddle the meaning of homophones – words like 'soar' and 'saw', which sound much the same but mean quite different things. So their problem seems to be the mirror image of the phonological dyslexic. The phonological dyslexic trips up on sounds and depends instead on the word's visual appearance. The surface dyslexic, in contrast, finds it difficult to remember what words look like, and depends too heavily on working out their meaning through rules about letter–sound relationships.

We mention these different forms of acquired dyslexia in adults because they have been the inspiration for a number of recent detailed descriptions of individual children with reading problems. The basic idea behind all these studies is that there is a connection between the two kinds of 'dyslexia'. Children who are 'developmental dyslexics' may be like adults who are acquired dyslexics. If they are – if, that is, there are some children with reading difficulties who read in the same way as phonological dyslexics and others who are exactly like surface dyslexics – then here surely would be evidence that 'dyslexia' in children is a distinctive condition. If they are exactly like the distinctive groups which suffer from various types of 'acquired dyslexia', then they too must belong to distinctive groups.

This would be a good argument but for one thing. As we have already said it is not just a matter of proving backward readers to be curious cases: they must also be shown to be 'curiouser' than other children. This means that we have to show not only that these children are like acquired dyslexics in certain ways, but also that in just these same ways they are quite unlike normal children. Thus comparisons between poor readers and acquired dyslexics should also include details about the skills and the behaviour of normal children. Otherwise one will have no guarantee that the studies have anything to do with 'dyslexia' at all. The child whose progress in learning to read is smooth and untroubled might none the less at various stages show just the same oddities as the child who is said to be dyslexic.

Many recent attempts to link the two types of 'dyslexia' have failed to take this precaution. One example is a study done in Oxford by Christine Temple and John Marshall. They looked at the interesting case of an intelligent 17-year-old girl whose reading and spelling skills at that time hovered around the nine- and ten-year level and who had always had difficulties with written language. This girl, they thought, was remarkably like an adult phonological dyslexic. She was not very good at reading nonsense syllables, she made so-called 'derivational' and 'visual' errors ('height' for 'high' and 'achieve' for 'attractive'), and she had difficulty with long but regular words, such as 'herpetology', which can in principle be read by using letter–sound rules. Like phonological dyslexics, she seemed to stumble over letter–sound rules.

However, her spelling was different. She could, for example, write the kind of nonsense word which caused her immense difficulty in reading. The authors puzzled over this but returned to the similarities between her reading and that of the phonological dyslexic. They concluded that those similarities were strong enough for them to claim that they have found an analogue in childhood of phonological dyslexia. The girl's condition, they argued, has the 'same functional architecture' as that of the adult phonological dyslexic.

The study is careful, sensitive and provocative. But we must question its conclusions. The trouble is that the authors did not consider normal, typical children. They did not seem to wonder whether the same things would have been done by children of nine and ten years who read and spell normally for their age. On the face of it, it seems likely that many nine- and ten-year-olds would have found it hard to read words like 'herpetology' and 'hectographic', or nonsense words like 'korp' and 'wute'. Nor is it all that inconceivable that these same young normal readers would also have been prone to the derivational and visual errors which this particular backward reader produced. And the fact – apparently surprising to the authors – that the girl found it easier to use phonological rules when she spelled than when she was trying to read is not a surprise if one considers the evidence about reading and spelling in normal children. They often show this interesting discrepancy (as chapter 5 amply demonstrated).

Exactly the same problem beset another closely similar attempt to link 'developmental' with 'acquired' dyslexia conducted in London by Max Coltheart together with several other colleagues. Here the analogy was with surface dyslexia. The study concerned a 16½-year old girl of average intelligence but with grave problems with reading and spelling, as she read and spelled words roughly at the level of a typical nine- to ten-year-old. When the investigators looked more closely at her mistakes they decided that she had much the same difficulties as surface dyslexics. She found regular words easier than irregular words such as 'gauge' and 'debt'. Her difficulty with irregular words was then pinpointed with the help of a particularly ingenious test. They asked her to judge whether pairs of written words sounded the same as each other. Some of these words included irregular words like 'sew': the girl had to judge whether the two words 'sew' and 'so' sounded the same. Other pairs contained words that could both be called regular: 'hair' and 'hare' is the example which the authors give us: both words can be read on the basis of accepted spelling rules.

The girl made many more mistakes with the pairs which included irregular words. She was not at all happy with the words which transgressed normal spelling rules. Another similarity between her and the typical surface dyslexic was that she often read words in slightly the wrong way ('beer' for 'bear'), and subsequent questions showed that she really thought that the word meant what she had said. This is also something that surface dyslexics do.

The authors of this study concluded that they had found a developmental surface dyslexic, but we must hesitate once again. In this case too we have no guarantee that the girl's mistakes really were unusual. In fact there are reasonable grounds for thinking that they were quite typical for someone at her stage of reading. Children tend to find irregular words harder to read and write than regular ones.[2] The most striking thing about this girl's reading – her difficulty with irregular words – is something which can be found in the vast majority of children, both with and without reading problems. The real question is whether her difficulty with irregular words was particularly pronounced, and the study has no answer to this question.

Recently (with the help of Lawrence Impey) we took advantage of the fact that both of these girls read at approximately the 10-year-old level. We got together a group of school children, none of whom was a backward reader. Being around 10 years old, they were at the same reading level as the girls studied by Temple and Marshall and by Coltheart and his colleagues. We gave our children the bulk of the tests which both sets of experimenters had given to their cases, as we wanted to see how unusual the two girls actually were. The answer was that neither turned out to be all that untypical. In fact the average child in our group made the same sort of mistakes and nearly as many. Some made just as many of them as did the 'surface' dyslexic studied by Coltheart and his colleagues, having much the same difficulty with irregular words, and making as many 'regularization' errors as she did.

We found a slightly different picture when we compared the same children to Temple and Marshall's 'phonological dyslexic'. On the whole, our children made precisely the same kind of mistakes – visual paralexias, derivational errors, nonsense words more difficult to read than real ones – as she. But she did make more of these mistakes than our children did on average. Nevertheless a minority of our children, were like her – the same difficulty with nonsense words, the same sort of derivational errors and visual paralexias – on all these measures. She was not unique, and since her mistakes can be found in children who read perfectly normally for their age, they cannot have much to do with the reason for her difficulties with reading. So, our study shows two things. The first is that the reports on these two cases tell us nothing about the reasons for the girl's difficulties, and the second is that normal children (and backward readers too) do vary: some read in different ways than others. In fact, the real value of the measures that we have just been discussing might be to demonstrate differences among children at every level of reading. That would be extremely valuable, but it would be a far cry from establishing the existence of a group of children at the bottom of the reading ladder whose mistakes are bizarre and unique.

One ironic point about the so-called 'surface dyslexic' was that despite being said to use phonological codes she, like Temple and Marshall's case, was rather bad at reading nonsense words. Yet adult surface dyslexics are not meant to have any particular difficulty with phonological tasks of this sort. Once again we are faced with an apparent phonological difficulty in a backward reader, and it is interesting to see that some other people who were also looking at the possible connection between acquired and developmental dyslexia have come across exactly the same problem. Alan Baddeley and V.J. Lewis at Cambridge and Nick Ellis and T.R. Miles at Bangor were concerned with an analogy with deep dyslexia. They did not make the analogy in the first place but were responding to a suggestion made by Anthony Jorm that deep dyslexia and 'developmental dyslexia' are the same thing.[3] They themselves were in some doubt about Jorm's idea and in the end rejected it.

They got together a group of backward readers who were 13 years old, but three years behind in reading. The Cambridge/ Bangor group did three experiments. The only one to produce any difference between the 'dyslexics' and the 10-year-old normal children with the same reading levels (the reading age match) employed a technique which has cropped up several times already in this book. The children were given lists of nonsense words to read, in order to test their skill with phonological rules, and also lists of real words. The backward readers read the real words as well as the normal children, but fell behind quite dramatically with the nonsense words.

This does not mean that the backward readers were similar to deep dyslexics who on the whole cannot read nonsense words at all. The backward readers managed to read more than half their list of nonsense words correctly. In fact it was this difference between the two groups of 'dyslexics' which struck the investigators most forcibly, and their justified response to their own results was that the analogy between deep and 'developmental dyslexia' is not right. But the negative side to this conclusion should not distract us from the fact that there was a real difference with the nonsense words which takes exactly the same form as that discovered by Uta Frith and Maggie Snowling. Thus the main thing to have come out of these attempts to make a connection between backward readers and acquired dyslexics is something that we knew already. Confirmation that backward readers are at a disadvantage when they have to dissect words into sounds is useful, but it does not knock down the idea of a continuum. On the contrary, it fits in well with the notion of a continuum of sensitivity to words' constituent sounds.

However, there is one study in this genre which does throw up a pattern of reading unlike anything that we have discussed so far and indeed unlike anything that we ourselves have seen in any normal children. The study was an Australian one and done by Margot Prior and M. McCorriston. They were interested in a form of acquired dyslexia, which goes under a variety of names, where the main symptom is the need to spell each word out letter by letter in order to read it. This happens to a number of people afflicted by brain damage, and it is worth noting that these people usually can write words without a great deal of trouble. But their reading is necessarily very slow and it is radically affected by the length of the words that they are given to read: the longer the word, the more likely they are to misread it.

Prior and McCorriston found an 11-year-old whose reading and spelling were at the level of a typical 6½-year-old, and who also read words letter by letter. She too found longer words considerably harder to read than short ones, and when the two experimenters took steps to prevent her from spelling the words out before deciding what they were she hardly read any of them. However, the two experimenters were modest about their analogy with adult dyslexic patients because the girl also had a great deal of difficulty in writing words, and that on the whole is not true of the adults who read words letter by letter.

But in our opinion this does not matter at all. The most striking thing is that here is a girl who seems to be doing the opposite of what most backward readers and indeed most young children do. Instead of treating written words as wholes she has to attend to every single letter in them. It seems very likely that this is one example of a problem which is a genuinely distinctive one and not part of any continuum. We cannot say so with certainty and we should have to check this by looking at normal children too: once again we are dealing with a study which left out this essential precaution. But the evidence that we reviewed in chapter 5 makes it probable that the typical 6½-year-old child does not read in this way.

One would like to know more about this girl. Perhaps the reason for her resorting to letter-by-letter reading was that she could not take in or remember the visual appearance of words or of common sequences of letters. She might in other words be, in the Boder sense, an extreme dyseidetic. It certainly would be good to know how she fares with other visual problems which do not involve written words. She might have a general perceptual problem. We cannot tell, but at any rate on her own this one girl is justification enough for the use of the single-case method (but with the proper controls, please). She does not belong to the continuum for which we have been arguing right through this book.


## Notes

1 The analogy between acquired and developmental dyslexia implies that developmental dyslexia is the result of some specific oddity in the brain. However, that is a completely different issue from the question of the continuum. It could be the case that some children who are backward readers suffer from some particular oddity in their brain (and recent, as yet unpublished, work by Norman Geschwind and his colleagues suggests that in some cases they do), but that its effect is to put backward readers right at the bottom of some continuum, such as that of phonological ability. In that case their reasons for being backward in reading would be quite distincitve, but these children would none the less still be part of a continuum.
2 The research reported in Sue Robertson's 1984 Oxford D. Phil thesis establishes this beyond doubt.
3 We refer here to Jorm's 1979 paper.

# 7

# Two ways of teaching backward readers

We began this book with the intention of putting forward some clear practical recommendations, and we hoped to give good scientific reasons for them. Lynette Bradley has developed two methods – two ways of helping backward readers which, we think, work particularly well. One involves increasing the children's phonological skills. The other is a variant of the type of teaching which is often called multisensory. In this chapter we shall say why we consider these two methods to be so effective, and then in the final chapter we shall describe each of them in enough detail to be used by other people.

Given our conclusions in the last five chapters, we think that any successful way of teaching backward readers should (1) foster their awareness of sounds in words, (2) show them how to make generalizations about spelling, (3) emphasize and demonstrate the connections between reading and spelling and between the phonological and visual sides of reading and writing, and (4) cater for the fact that different backward readers may set about reading in different ways.

Establishing ways of helping backward readers is only one of our practical aims. The other is to prevent children from ever becoming backward readers in the first place. We want to find ways of preparing them before they go to school, so that by the time they get there they will cope with reading and writing perfectly well. In our opinion, there are good reasons for thinking that the first of our two methods, increasing phonological skills, is a good preventative step to take, as well as an extremely effective tool for teaching older children who have already emerged as backward readers, whereas our second method probably only works with older children. We shall consider the two methods separately.

## Increasing phonological skills

Our simplest and most obvious starting point is the child's awareness of sounds in words. We have shown how a child's skill with these sounds plays an important part in his success in reading and in spelling. This means that we ought to consider how to remove the often striking insensitivity of backward readers to these sounds. There are really two questions here. One is how to make them more sensitive and the second is whether doing so helps backward readers over their difficulties.

Several people have tried to improve children's awareness of sounds and some also looked at the effect of this kind of teaching on reading and spelling. We now know that it is possible and even quite easy to make children more aware of the sounds within words. In Sweden Ake Olofsson and Ingvar Lundberg showed this when they took a group of 6–7-year-old children (in Sweden children do not go to school till the age of 7 years) and taught them about words' constituent sounds. They did this with a number of ingenious games. One with a distinct local flavour involved a troll who could only say words in a disjointed way, one sound at a time and with marked intervals between each sound. In others, the children had to categorize pictures by the beginning sounds in their names or to blend separate sounds into words. Some of these children were given these games in a particularly structured way; the exact methods that the teacher used were determined quite explicitly by the experimenters. Other children were given the same games, but the teacher had more freedom to determine when and how these games were conducted. This whole programme went on for three or four sessions a week for between six and eight weeks.

These games did have an effect. At the end of the study the children were given a number of tests of 'phonological awareness', where they had to break up words into their constituent sounds and also to put together sounds that they heard separately to make a single word. The children who had taken part in the programme were clearly superior to other children who had not. Those who went through the structured version of the programme did particularly well. Thus it is possible to show children how a word can be divided into sounds and to do so before they begin to learn to read (though one should be cautious here: what is true of seven-year-old Swedish children may not be true of four-year-old English children). This is encouraging, because it means that such extra help ought to lead to more successful reading. There is now quite a lot of evidence that it does.

## What are the effects on their reading of teaching children about sounds?

There are two ways of looking at this question. One, the tougher and purer way, is to see what happens when children are taught only about sounds without any explicit reference to the alphabet or to written words. Would this sort of teaching help them to learn to read? According to our ideas it should. The second, a rather weaker test of our notions, is to look at programmes for teaching reading which emphasize the so-called 'phonic' approach. There are, of course, many such programmes and there have been several attempts to look at how effective they are. This information is important but it is not a stringent test of our ideas, because inevitably these phonic programmes involve a great deal more than teaching about sounds: the children see the written words as well and probably build up memories of what they look like. In principle it ought to be possible to control for these other experiences, but in practice this has not happened.

*Teaching phonological awareness alone*

To some extent we have already dealt with the first of these two approaches. In chapter 4 we described how the work of Goldstein, of Fox and Routh and of Williams established that extra coaching in detecting sounds in words does help children to learn to read. In that chapter too we began to describe our own training study, which showed that merely training children how to categorize words on the basis of their common sounds had the effect of making them better readers and spellers too. We shall be returning in more detail to this study later on in this chapter.

These are results of the utmost practical importance. We know now that one very good way of helping a child to read is to make him more sensitive to sounds in words, and we also have a very good theoretical reason why this should be so. But, since we are at the moment dealing with strictly practical issues, we are immediately faced with another question. Is it enough simply to give a child extra coaching about the sounds in words, or should this additional teaching be combined with explicit instruction about written words *at the same time*? Should you simply, for example, show a child that 'cat' and 'cup' are words which start with the same sound, or should you also at that moment teach him that both words start with the same alphabetic letter?

*Phonic teaching*

Phonic teaching methods involve both things of course and there is no doubt that these methods by and large are successful. Some of their most significant successes have been with backward readers. Several studies point this way. In England, Beve Hornsby and Tim Miles looked at the work of three different remedial schools for children in difficulty with learning to read. These schools used rather different methods from each other, but one of the things they had in common was their emphasis on sounds and the relationship between these and alphabetic letters. (Another was their emphasis on structured, sequential programmes.) Under this type of regime most of the children made quite reasonable progress, and so the schools' 'phonic' methods gave every sign of being successful. However, we cannot be completely sure of this. The study would have been more convincing if the children's progress had been compared to, and shown to be better than, that of others who had not had the benefit of the educational programmes in question.

One study which does include this sort of comparison is the one by Rachel Gittelman and Ingrid Feingold in New York. They divided a number of backward readers into two groups, one of which was given a systematic phonic programme over a period of four months, whereas the rest were given the same amount of extra attention, but this took the form of 'non-specific tutoring in other subjects'. By the end of the four months the first group of children was much better at reading (roughly twelve months ahead on average) than the other, and it remained better. When the children were visited again two months and then eight months after the teaching had stopped the children in the first group were still well ahead of the others.

Other studies have produced much the same kind of result, and the obvious conclusion from them, that teaching reading by emphasizing the association between sounds and letters does work particularly well, seems to have been widely accepted by people who do teach backward readers. In 1983 Sandhya Naidoo reviewed a large number of the different remedial methods which are in use at the moment and showed quite clearly that they all concentrate on sounds: 'All employ a phonic approach and all eschew whole word methods'(p.282). Of course, this fits in well with our general idea about the importance of the awareness of sounds. But we ought perhaps to hesitate a little before concluding that successful teaching, or even successful teaching of backward readers, is just a matter of sounds and of nothing else.

For one thing, if the answer lies in phonic methods and if these are used so widely, why do so many backward readers remain poor at reading? That is one sobering reason for caution. Another is that some phonic methods are more successful than others. This was established in 1983 by A.B. Branwhite who gave two different phonic programmes to different groups of backward readers. One programme was very carefully planned in the same way as the programmes which Hornsby and Miles looked at. The children went through it in an explicit series of steps, the order of which was rigidly determined beforehand, and each step led to the next. In the other programme the teaching was still about sounds, but without nearly as much structure. The first group prospered far more than the second. We have to recognize that it is not just training in sounds that is important. We must think about what goes with it as well. Branwhite's study reminds us of this problem, but it does not solve it. There were too many differences between the two programmes which he looked at, and he made no attempt to compare the children's progress to that of others who had not had any extra help with letter–sound relationships. We cannot say whether the less successful of the two programmes had any effect or not.

The research on the effects of these and of other teaching methods has not been at all distinguished. When you want to know whether a particular experience helps children to learn to read, you obviously look at what happens when you give some children an added amount of this experience. But you also have to compare them to other children whom you see for the same amount of time, if possible with help from the same teachers, and whom you treat in exactly the same way and give the same material, *except* for the experience whose effects you want to test. The first group gets that, and the second does not. None of the studies which we have mentioned so far in this chapter got anywhere near doing this properly, and we have been hard put to it to find any study which makes this kind of stringent comparison. It is difficult to do, but essential none the less.

We know now that extra teaching just about sounds does eventually help a child to learn to read. We know too that there are reasonable grounds for thinking that phonic methods of teaching reading, which involve both sounds and written words, do help backward readers. But we cannot say anything coherent about how these methods work, about what is the best way to apply them, and we have no answer at all to our question whether the teaching of sounds on its own is enough or whether it works better when combined with instruction about alphabetic letters and written words. We must turn to studies which are more carefully constructed than those which we have described so far.

### Teaching sounds with the help of alphabetic letters – the first method

This brings us back to our training study which we described in chapter 4.[1] Of the two groups of children who were taught how to categorize words by their sounds, those who were also taught to embody these sounds in alphabetic plastic letters were many months ahead of the rest by the end of the project. The combination of these two experiences adds up to an extremely effective teaching method, and one that is obviously worth looking at more closely. The next chapter will give the details of the experiences which were given to the children in this strikingly successful group.

Why did they do so well? In chapter 4 we suggested that it was not just a matter of introducing letters, but of introducing them in a very specific way. Remember that the letters were plastic ones which meant that it was easily possible to remove one letter at a time and leave the rest of the word intact. This in turn meant that the children could change one written word into another (e.g. 'cat' to 'hat') simply by removing one letter and substituting another, all the while keeping the common letters untouched. We showed them how the words all contained a particular visual pattern (e.g. '-at') and we think that they learned the sequence of letters which words of this sort share. So we were teaching them about two kinds of category – the sounds and the visual patterns which the different words share with each other – at the same time.

We believe, although we must be clear that we are only

speculating at this point, that the method works well for two reasons. One is that it does improve the all important phonological skills and connects them tangibly to the alphabet. The second arises from some work which we described in chapter 5. There we showed that children who are just beginning to learn to read and write tend to treat what they learn about a written word's sounds and what they learn about its visual appearance as two separate things. This unnecessary separation is particularly pronounced in backward readers. Apply this discovery to categories, and you are faced with the possibility that children in general and backward readers in particular learn that there are words with common sounds and also that there are words with common sequences of letters, but that they do not at first associate these two kinds of categories with each other.

If this is so – and please remember that we are just speculating – the plastic letters helped the children to make this particular connection. The letters emphasized the visual patterns which the words had in common and at the same time we ourselves stressed that these words also shared a common sound. We taught the children how to categorize the same group of words in two ways at the same time and this might have shown them how to connect two different kinds of learning.

## The question of prevention

By prevention we mean the steps to be taken with children, long before they go to school, to stop any of them eventually turning out as backward readers. One obvious possibility would be to improve their awareness of sounds. Would this help children, who otherwise would have become backward readers, to learn to read quite normally when they arrive at school? It seems such a simple question, and at the same time such an important one, that it comes as something of a surprise to find that virtually nothing is known about it. In fact, virtually nothing is known about the question of prevention in general. It has been shockingly neglected.

The trouble, we think, has been that people have tended to link prevention with prediction. At first sight this may seem to be a reasonable connection. It seems obvious that you should be able to spot the child who risks becoming a backward reader before you take steps to help him. Otherwise you will end up helping the wrong child. So, the argument usually goes, you need ways of looking at two-, three- or four-year-old children and of predicting with considerable accuracy which of them are likely to learn to read more slowly than is warranted by their general intellectual level. The trouble is that so far no one has found an effective way of doing this. Although we can make a fairly accurate overall prediction about children's success in reading, given what we know about their intelligence and their language (on the whole the most advanced pre-school children later turn out to be the most successful readers), there will be exceptions, and our problem is that there is no known way of detecting these exceptions in advance with accuracy.

We found this difficulty even with our own measures of sensitivity to rhyme and alliteration. We had shown in our large-scale longitudinal study that there is a good overall relationship between the scores which children manage on these measures at four and five years of age and their success in reading three to four years later (even allowing for differences in intelligence and in several other factors as well). But what about individual children? We looked at all the children in our study whose reading levels were well below what one would expect given their age and intelligence, and the question that we asked was whether we could have detected these children in our original tests of rhyme and alliteration three or four years earlier. The answer was that we should have picked up some of them (roughly 25 per cent), but that we should have missed the rest, and we should also have predicted, quite wrongly, that some of the children who actually turned out well were to become backward readers.[2]

We had hoped for a better result, but though we were disappointed we knew of no other measures which would have worked any better than ours did. So what is one to do? There are two possible courses. One is to take the line that there is no way of preventing reading difficulties without an accurate tool for predicting them in advance and to give up any hope of prevention until such a tool is discovered. The other, less drastic possibility which we favour, is to keep the two issues, prediction and prevention, well apart. We have done this already in the opening chapter. There we argued that you only need to know how to predict the backward readers if they really do form a distinct group with a very distinct problem. If, on the other hand, the same factors influence reading in all children, good and backward readers alike, there will be no need for this elusive tool. What helps backward readers will help all other children as well. We do not have to worry about selecting a special group to be treated in a special way, because what helps one child will help all children.

Everything we have discussed in this book points to this sort of continuum. To return to rhyme and alliteration, here are things which backward readers find particularly difficult, to be sure. But our large study showed that these skills play their part at all levels of reading. On the whole children who detect rhymes particularly well will do better than one would expect (given their IQ) at learning to read, just as those who are insensitive to rhyme will do worse than expected. Our recommendation then is very simple. Make sure that children have every possible experience with nursery rhymes, and verses and word-games in the years before they go to school. Do everything possible to show them how the words which they speak and hear can be broken up into syllables and smaller sound segments.

How to do this effectively is another question. We know of no good research to answer it. But we can appeal again to Chukovsky who has demonstrated at least that playing with words and their sounds is something which children do quite naturally and with obvious enjoyment. Not only that. This is the sort of thing which children seem to like doing with other people. They tell parents about the rhymes that they have produced and they enjoy hearing their parents' verses. It is an extraordinarily interesting part of the natural social interplay between children and their parents, and one about which we know far too little. We need more information, but we can be confident that parents could go a long way towards removing the problem of reading difficulties by encouraging their children to play with sounds in the years before school.

## Multi-sensory teaching – the second method

The 'multi-sensory' idea has a long and honourable history. It is a rag-bag term and it has been applied to many very disparate methods of teaching children to read. When we use it we mean ways of teaching children which stress all the different channels – vision, hearing, touch and movement – involved in reading and writing and which stress them all at the same time.

We are interested in the multi-sensory idea because of the very explicit connection it makes between the different activities involved in reading and spelling. One of the main problems of backward readers (apart from their difficulties with sounds) is, as we have already seen, a certain disconnection between reading and spelling and between the visual and auditory sides of learning to read and spell. Multi-sensory methods are *par excellence* tools for forging links between these things.

Maria Montessori was one of the first to argue for a close link between learning to read and to write. Her enthusiasm for making this connection stemmed from her general ideas about early education. Her principal idea was that children learn best when they learn actively: 'The fundamental technique in education is this – that the child should always be active and allowed to choose his occupation, and thus give form to his actions.'[3] She argued that the easiest and most obvious way for young children to be active was by moving: 'This principle of movement should be carried right through education: so that in all its manifestations there should be this union between the child's ego and his actions.'

Her rather high-flown language conceals some concrete suggestions about learning to read. Montessori made a strong claim for the importance of writing letters and words while at the very same time learning about their sounds. She thought that the child should trace letters and, while he did so, the teacher should say what their sounds were. She emphasized the cues that the children got from tracing by giving them alphabetic letters made out of sandpaper. This gave the letters a distinctive feel and made it easy for the children to do what she wanted, which was 'to touch over the alphabetical signs as though they were writing'. Later the child had to practise with the letters on his own. In Montessori's own words:

> The child then touches the letters by himself over and over again . . . and in this way he establishes the movements necessary for tracing the alphabetical signs. At the same time he retains the visual image of the letter. This process forms the preparation not only for writing but also for reading because it is evident that when the child touches the letters he performs the movement corresponding to the writing of them, and at the same time when he recognises them by sight he is reading the alphabet.

Notice the insistence on the child being active, and also the emphasis on links between vision, movement and, by implication, sound as well. Montessori was concerned with connections.

So were many other people but usually for different reasons. Samuel Orton, as we have already noted, was one of the most enthusiastic supporters of the idea of multi-sensory teaching, and in a way was one of the method's pioneers. Here are his reasons:

> If confusion in the direction of reading forms the obstacle to proper association of the printed word with its meaning, the obvious corrective measure should be aimed at training for consistent direction in reading. One

very valuable aid immediately suggests itself here, and that is the inclusion of kinaesthetic directional training in the building up of associations. In general the re-education method which we propose may be said to be based on training for simultaneous association of visual, auditory and kinaesthetic fields, i.e. tracing and sounding the visually presented word and maintaining consistent direction by following the letters with the finger during sound synthesis of syllables and words.

Orton's theory was quite different from Montessori's. She was concerned with the importance of action in general and movement in particular. He (as we saw in chapter 3) was worried about children's confusions over the direction of letters and words. But in a way he went beyond this specific concern with 'strephosymbolia', just as Montessori went beyond her notions about movement. He began with the idea of kinaesthetic training as a cure for directional problems and ended with a technique which included kinaesthetic experiences and teaching about the visual shape of letters and words and about sounds in words all at the same time. The starting points for these two pioneers were very different and yet in the end their practical suggestions were much the same.

Orton himself was not a teacher, and he developed these ideas about multi-sensory methods together with a colleague, Anna Gillingham, who was. She in turn worked with Bessie Stillman who had herself suffered grave reading difficulties. Between the three of them, neurologist, teacher and erstwhile poor reader, they devised a scheme which is variously known as the Orton–Gillingham or as the Gillingham–Stillman method.

Orton and his colleagues developed a programme which was both precise and highly structured. They emphasized the importance of the auditory and kinaesthetic information, because they hoped that these would make up for what they saw as the vagaries of the backward reader's visual system. First they taught letter–sound correspondences introducing each new 'phonogram' (letter–sound pair) through eight steps or 'linkages', and then concentrated on making sure that the children could analyse and put together the sounds to make words. Linkages 7 and 8 were the translation of sounds into letter names (oral spelling) or into letter forms (written spelling), a technique which they called 'Simultaneous Oral Spelling'.

> The pupil says a word, spells it orally and then writes it, naming each letter aloud as his hand forms it. Every strephosymbolic speller should study his spelling of particular words in this way. . . . It is very common for a child to spell words correctly, if he says the letters even subvocally. . . . The three-fold association of visual, auditory and kinesthetic must never be neglected.

The last person in our list of people who espoused the multi-sensory approach is Grace Fernald. Her approach was different in various ways from the two we have just described. To begin with, it was not 'phonic' as it depended on whole words and on syllables rather than on breaking these down into smaller units of sound. Another difference was that unlike the Orton method (and a large number of other teaching methods specially devised for backward readers) it did not consist of a rigidly fixed sequence of steps.

Fernald gave movement a central role. She argued that kinaesthetic cues play an important part in linking the visual and spoken form of the word. Her method took the following form. The children thought of words which they themselves wanted to learn to write (an important move this, partly because it keeps the children's interest up and partly because their vocabulary does vary considerably and one needs to start at least with words that they know), and the teacher wrote the words on a card, usually putting them in a meaningful sentence. The child then traces the word with a finger, *à la* Montessori, intoning each syllable of the word as he traces it. He repeats this until he can write the word without looking at it. First he looks at each word, and then says and writes it from memory. The method is a 'simultaneous' one, because as he writes the syllables in the word he also pronounces them. Fernald's idea was that in doing all this the child learns smooth motor patterns for groups of letters, and at the same time links them to particular syllables.

So here we have three rather elegant variations on the same theme, and now we can consider what the three have in common. There are two common elements. One is the explicit way in which the three link the different aspects of written language. They connect reading with writing, visual with auditory perception (and visual with auditory memory), and these with familiar patterns of movment. The second is their heavy emphasis on the importance of movement, and this surely needs some explanation. Why should movement play an important part in learning to read? Reading, after all, is a matter of taking in and deciphering linguistic information. It is difficult at first to understand what role the movements of our hands and arms could have to do with that. Let us see what we can make of the convictions of Montessori, Orton and Fernald.

## Simultaneous Oral Spelling – the second method

There is at least one powerful reason why children might learn more about written words with the help of systematic experience of writing these words. We have already discussed the importance of 'chunking' and this may be yet another form of chunking. Children may learn a particular sequence of letters by becoming familiar with the pattern of movements which they make when they write the sequence.

There was little evidence on this question until quite recently, which was odd because the question itself had been in the air for a long time. Now at any rate we do have some direct evidence, and it does suggest that movement can help backward readers to remember sequences of letters. The evidence was provided by Charles Hulme in some work that he did in Oxford. He showed a group of backward readers and a group of normal readers (using the reading-age match) strings of letters, and asked the children to remember them. He asked all the children to look at the letters (which some of the time were plastic) in several of the strings and to trace around each one with a finger. He also asked them simply to look at other strings of letters.

Tracing helped all the children to remember the letters better, but it helped the backward readers more than the other children. There is obviously something about movement that is important to backward readers when they have to remember alphabetic letters. This is a most important piece of evidence, and it gives us a possible rationale for multi-sensory methods. They may work – if they do – simply because they involve a heavy emphasis on movements.

However, we cannot be sure from this one experiment on children's memory for meaningless strings of letters that the experience of learning particular patterns of movement will help the far more complex business of learning to read. That is just a speculation, and so is the answer to another broader question. Do the multi-sensory methods which we have just described actually work?

It sounds a simple enough question to settle. Just set up a comparison between children taught in a multi-sensory way and others who were not. But this kind of large-scale comparison of children taught by different teachers in different ways in different classrooms and often in different schools is difficult to do properly. Too many other influences are at work, and it is often quite impossible to do anything about them. One only has to think of the teachers' justified and necessary enthusiasm for a new and promising method to realize that this in itself might be a factor. It may be the enthusiasm and not the method itself that works. One of the other problems is that it is often difficult to be sure that the children who are being compared are the same in every important respect at the start of the project. One does one's best, but since all the important factors are not known one cannot be sure that all have been controlled.

We think that there is another way to settle the issue. It is to compare not children, but words. You have, let us say, two teaching methods which you want to compare. You have a set of words which you want the children to learn to read and write. So you teach these words to all the children, but teach them different words in different ways. Then you see which words they learn and remember better. It is an extremely effective way of comparing teaching methods because it avoids all the problems of differences between teachers and also between children taught by the different methods.

Lynette Bradley did this kind of study to test the effectiveness of a variant of the method of 'Simultaneous Oral Spelling'.[4] Her method was the same as Gillingham and Stillman's in some respects, but different in others. She too got the children to name each letter as they wrote words. However she taught them to do so even if they did not know the letters already. (She did this because of her previous experience that this did not matter so long as the child was writing words which he wanted to write, as Fernald had suggested.)

She wanted to find out whether this was an effective way of teaching backward readers. She also wanted to know why, if it works, it does help them. She formed a corpus of 16 words which she taught to a group of backward readers. These words were 'sew, buy, toe, won, calf, suit, ache, sign, type, tear, suit, cute, laugh, tough, chief and juice'. At the beginning of the project none of the children could spell any of the 16 words. She taught each child 12 of the 16 words over a period of four days. These 12 words were in turn divided into three sets of four. Each set was taught in a different manner. So the study compared three teaching methods, and it is to those that we must now turn.

The first of these methods was the one at issue. It was Bradley's version of 'Simultaneous Oral Spelling'. Each child was taught 4 out of the 12 words in much the same way as Gillingham and Stillman taught words to their children, but without teaching the letter–sound correspondences first:

The word to be learned is presented to the child on a small card. The experimenter then reads the word to the child, and the child repeats it. The child then writes the word saying the name of each letter as it is written. When the word has been written, the child says the word once more, and then checks to see that the word has been written correctly. After this the word is covered, and the whole process is repeated twice.

The technique involves at least three major things – visual information (seeing the word), auditory/orthographic information (spelling out the letters) and, thirdly, writing movements. Bradley's aim, with the help of the other two methods, was to find out something about the relative importance of these various elements.

The second method was called 'Visual and Motor'. Each child was taught to read and write four words in this way. The method was identical to the first apart from omitting the auditory/orthographic element. Although the children named each word, they did not spell them out as they wrote them (this method was similar to Fernald's).

The children learned the other four words by the third

*The child writes the word saying the name of each letter as it is written.*

method, which was called 'Visual and Auditory'. Again this was exactly like the first method but for one thing. This time the motor element was left out. The children no longer wrote the words. Instead they were given letters written on small cards and had to lay them out, naming each letter as they did so.

That was how the 12 words were taught; the final untaught 4 words acted as a control. The question behind the experiment was whether teaching the children about the words would help them, after an interval, to remember how to read and write them, and whether there would be any difference in the effectiveness of the three different methods. Bradley tested the children's ability to read and spell these words three times, once on the last day (the fifth day) of the teaching, once again two weeks later and for the last time after a further two weeks.

Four weeks after the teaching ended a clear difference had emerged between the three teaching methods. The backward readers remembered how to spell the words taught by the method of 'Simultaneous Oral Spelling' very well: even after so long an interval they could spell 58 per cent without a mistake. The figures for the other two methods were considerably lower: they were between 30 and 35 per cent. So by far and away the most successful method for the backward readers was the one pioneeered by Gillingham and Stillman which emphasizes so many aspects of reading and writing at the same time. Dropping the auditory/orthographic element ('Visual–Motor' method) or the motor element ('Visual–Auditory' method) very nearly halves the backward readers' chance of learning how to spell a word correctly.

What is the reason for this effect? Why should multi-sensory methods be a particular help to backward readers? We can no longer say that it is just a matter of emphasizing movement. This, the simplest possible explanation, seems to be ruled out by the discovery that the 'Visual–Motor' method did not help backward readers nearly so much as the fully fledged 'Simultaneous Oral Spelling' technique.

Our answer harks back to the second of the main

conclusions with which we began this chapter, that there is a pronounced separation between reading and spelling among backward readers and less of one among normal readers at the same general level of reading. We think that multi-sensory and 'Simultaneous Oral Spelling' works by helping backward readers to organize and to connect their existing skills more effectively, as Gillingham and Stillman suggested. The method does make very explicit connections between reading and spelling, and in a way 'Simultaneous Oral Spelling' is a misnomer as the technique involves not just spelling but reading as well and in close conjunction. The child has to read the word and say it before he writes it. The two activities are put together as closely as possible. Therefore it seems quite likely that the technique works by making the child see that reading and writing are, to quote Uta Frith, 'two sides of the same coin'.

How can we find out whether this idea is right? Our only evidence so far is that removing any element in the complex combination of activities involved in the technique seems to make it much less successful, and we need more evidence of the sort to be found in the Bradley study. What, for instance, would happen if the reading element were removed – if, for example, we carried out the 'Simultaneous Oral Spelling' method step by step apart from making sure that the child never read the word that he was writing? We expect that this version would hardly work at all with backward readers like Mark (though it would with other children) because it could not foster the connection between reading and spelling.

Another way of looking at our idea would be to go back to the discrepancy between reading and spelling which we reported in chapter 5. Remember that we found that backward readers often read some words which they could not spell and also spelled some words which they could not read. If our ideas about 'Simultaneous Oral Spelling' are right, then the technique should not only improve reading and spelling but should also cut down on the number of these discrepancies. That, in fact, would be the crucial test of our notion that this impressive teaching method helps backward readers to marshall the skills which they already possess but which up till now have not helped them much. It could prove a useful alternative for children who find phonological strategies difficult. We like the idea of a teaching method which helps a child in difficulty to live up to his own talents and shows him how impressive these talents really are.[5]

## Notes

1  This is the study described in our 1983 *Nature* paper and, in detail, in our 1985 monograph.
2  There is a chapter on this side of our results in our 1985 monograph.
3  All the Montessori quotations in this chapter come from the excellent biography by E.M. Standing.
4  This study by Lynette Bradley was published in 1981 in *Developmental Medicine and Child Neurology*.
5  We have not discussed training which concentrates purely on movement or the effects of drugs, partly because we think that nothing of importance has been established about either approach and partly because they fall well outside our theoretical framework. Rachel Gittelman wrote a good review chapter which deals with both topics in the book edited by Michael Rutter (1983).

# 8

# The two methods in practice

Now we shall describe Bradley's two teaching methods in some detail. In the last chapter we produced some strong evidence that they do help children. We presented these methods separately though we think that, in practice, a judicious mix of the two works best. The actual form of the mix depends on the individual child, and it will always be up to the teacher to decide which parts to emphasize and which to play down. In this chapter we shall describe the methods first, again separately. Then we shall give examples of the way in which they were given to some very different children to show how the same two methods can be, and actually have to be, combined in rather different ways in different cases.

## The first method – improving phonological skills

The first method was designed to do two things. One was to make children more aware of the sounds shared by quite different words, and the other to give them the idea that words with common sounds often share the same spelling patterns too. That was the reason for using the plastic alphabetic letters. They made it possible to change one word to another (e.g. 'light' to 'fight') and at the same time to keep intact the spelling sequence (in this case '-igh') which represents the common sound.

Here is the way that we used this method in the study which we originally described in chapter 4. When the letters were introduced the children had already had quite a lot of experience of putting words which had common sounds into the same category. We do not think that this prior experience is necessary, but it does help children to make faster progress with this method.

We started by asking them to choose a word from one of the categories which they already knew. Let us say that this was 'hen'. Then the child was encouraged to make this word with the plastic letters. Once this was done, the teacher asked the child to form another word from the same category. Invariably the child would at first scrap the whole word ('hen') and proceed to form the next word ('pen') from scratch. But as time went on and word followed word, each with the same spelling pattern ('hen', 'men', 'pen', 'ten'), the child would begin to realize that there was a common letter sequence which did not have to be destroyed each time. He made for himself the important discovery that words which share a common sound often have a spelling sequence in common. The child would then begin to leave that sequence untouched and change only the letter or letters which symbolised the altered sound. The most important thing about this method was that it showed the child how groups of words which have sounds in common also often have sequences of letters in common too. The experience of changing one word to another word in the same group seems to us the best way to teach a child how to generalize from common sounds to common spelling patterns.

But that is not all. In our view the child should also learn that the same word can be put into sound categories in different ways and that these different ways are also represented by spelling. 'Pen', for example, may end the same way as 'hen' and 'men', but it begins the same way as 'pet' and 'peg'. So, having taught the child about the spelling pattern '-en', we now went on to the pattern 'pe-', using exactly the same method. Once again the child had to change one word formed by plastic letters into another and then into another; 'pen' to 'pet' to 'peg'. This taught the child not only about categorizing words by their first sounds, but also how a word

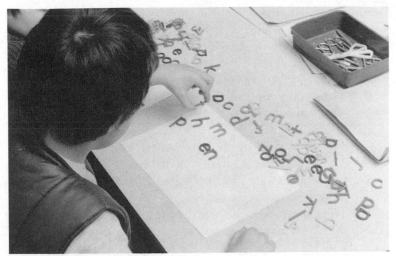

*Here the child changes hen to pen, ten, and men, discovering for himself that words which share a common sound often have a spelling sequence in common.*

like 'pen' can be categorized by its beginning as well as by its end sounds.

After this the categories became more sophisticated. The children discovered categories of words which had only a mid-sound connection (for example 'peg' with 'men' and 'bed'). Once the child had mastered categories like this he certainly knew a great deal about breaking words up into their constituent sounds and about spelling these constituents. It was not surprising that the children given this training in our study did so much better at reading and spelling than did the other children who received just as much attention.

## The second method – 'Simultaneous Oral Spelling'

This is a method which can be used to teach any kind of word however irregular it is and however difficult to put into the categories that we have just discussed. The method is easy enough to describe. There are six clear steps (with a possible seventh, although that depends on the word itself). The procedure is the same whether or not the child can read or write, and whether or not he is familiar with all the sound/symbol associations. However, care must be taken not to let the teaching become an exercise in rote learning. The steps are:

1   The child proposes the word which he wants to learn.
2   The teacher writes the word for him (or forms it with plastic letters).
3   The child then names the written word.
4   The child then writes the word himself, and *at the same time* names each alphabetic letter (using letter names) as he writes it.
5   Then he names the word again. He checks to see that the word has been written correctly by comparing it with the one written by the teacher. After that steps 2 – 5 are repeated three times over.[1]
6   The child practises the word (and any others) in this way for six consecutive days until eventually the child can write the word without looking at the original word written by the teacher. He may achieve this on the first day with some words, but more complex words take longer. When he can write the word without having to copy it the first stage of the teaching, at any rate as far as that word is concerned, is complete.

The next step depends, for obvious reasons, on the regularity of the word itself, but is usually possible and, in our view, always helpful.

7   The child learns with the help of plastic letters to generalize from that word to others which share the same sounds and the same spelling sequences.

## Individual children

We can now tell the story of some children who were taught with the help of one or both of these methods. But we must start with a caveat: these examples are not evidence. We have already provided all the evidence that we have for these two methods. Our reason for giving these examples is to illustrate what the methods involve with individual children, and nothing more.

## Tim

*The problem.* Our first example is a complex one. Tim was 10 years old when we first saw him, and he was sent to us then because he had made very little progress at school. We were not the first people that he had been sent to. From the age of five he had been seeing speech therapists because his speech was difficult to understand. The problem seemed at the time to be in his speech rather than in his language. He tended to substitute incorrect sounds for correct ones, very much in the way that much younger children do.

He had been tested in various ways before we met him first and we already knew that his intelligence was normal (IQ 97), but that he had fallen four years behind in reading. Our first impression was of a pleasant boy whose speech was immature and who seemed to have some general language difficulties as well. He was also obviously clumsy and his movements noticeably imprecise.

We looked at three things: (1) his spoken language, (2) his reading and writing, and (3) how he fared in tasks which involved little or no language.

*Spoken language.* We tape-recorded a session in which we got Tim to talk about various things. We asked him questions and got him to tell us a story. We also gave him our rhyme and alliteration tasks.

He seemed to have great difficulty in organizing what he wanted to say. His sentences were full of pauses and repetitions which seemed to us to take the form of a delaying tactic while he tried to think of what to say next. Here is a short extract from the session: / means a distinct pause, and (——) indicates speech sounds that were incomprehensible.

Uh. /. Yes (——). So now d/ at at at school (——) now
sometimes / an some o' my writing doesn't make sense
one line because I put per / (——) / the wrong word in /
because I couldn't even cofy / another word.

Here is part of his story.

Um, I um I was sitting / by the [*incomprehensible word*] by
my fire and suddenly the flying carpet / the carpet aside /
straight through the window and a / and um / and / I cut
my forehead / f and a / I am I / over the steeple over the
church and over the sea so land in (——) and my friend
was the Queen.

Of course without the necessary controls we cannot say for
certain that his language was definitely more poorly organized
than that of other children. We can, however, be certain that
his score on the rhyme and alliteration task was very low
indeed for someone of his age.

*Written language.* We confirmed that his scores on standardized
reading and spelling tests were at the level typical of a child of
between 6 and 6½ years. He tried to use context to help him
read, but his ability to decipher individual words was so poor
that his guesses were wild ones and usually led him far from
the real meaning of the passage. We also looked at his memory
for individual written words by showing one at a time for a
brief period and asking him to reproduce them for us. He was
less successful on this task than six-year-old children normally
are.

All in all his ability to read and to remember written words
was very poor.

*Other tasks.* We found two other kinds of tasks which gave him
great difficulty, and we suspect that the link between them is
that both involved much planning. One was a standard
Piagetian test – seriation – which involved arranging a graded
series of sticks in order from smallest to largest. Although this

is something a normally intelligent child can do by the age of seven or eight years, Tim could not manage this. The other task was drawing a man: on standard scores he did no better than a typical five-year-old child.

*Remediation.* It seemed to us that Tim had to be helped in a number of ways. In particular he needed to be taught about the sounds in words and how these are related to spelling. He also seemed to need practice in marshalling his words (and thoughts) when setting about writing a passage of prose.

We did not teach him ourselves but conferred with the remedial teacher at his school about his teaching programme. This teaching was arranged around stories which Tim had to make up. In each remedial session he was encouraged to make up a story. He and the teacher went through it sentence by sentence, and before he wrote each sentence, the teacher checked that he knew the spelling of each word by asking him to make them up one by one with plastic letters. When this had been done he wrote the sentence out, but it is important to note that as he wrote each word he also spelled it out. (In other words the teacher was using the 'Simultaneous Oral Spelling' method which we have just described.)

After this Tim had to choose one word in each sentence as the 'key' word. He set this word out once again in plastic letters, and then using the method described in the first section of this chapter the teacher showed him how to convert it into other words with similar sounds and spelling patterns.

*Tim's progress. After one month* an extract from the teacher's report read: 'Reading – has made progress, more confident but still sounds out any word not instantly recognized. Recognition of sounds very weak. Writing – much improved, spacing better, also punctuation. Spelling – is learning to group words and shows improvement with memory for spelling patterns'.

*After two months* the report read: 'Some improvement in fluency of reading and definite improvement in speech. Better sentence construction. Inaccuracies with basic phonics.'

*After five months* the report read: 'More confident. Gradual progress continues. Spelling – fewer errors, but still the weak link. Has a more confident approach to language and quite imaginative ideas – using better vocabulary.'

*After six months* his scores on standardized reading and spelling tests reached 8 years 6 months and 7 years 6 months respectively – an advance of two years in reading and one year in spelling. He wrote a poem at this time, and a corrected version is given here.

Tim wrote this poem for his teacher.

*Tom*

*The problem.* We now turn to the case of a young boy with similar but not so severe difficulties. He was a bright boy of 7½ years who had made no progress at all in reading which, given his obvious intelligence, was a surprise to his parents

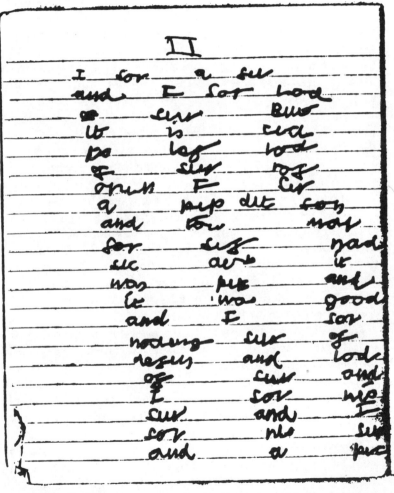

*Tom knew that he had to leave a space between each written word, but he could not write the actual words.*

and to his teacher. We shall see how in his case intervention at an early stage had a much happier outcome.

He was clumsy and his speech was slightly disorganised. He had no sense of the sounds in words. He could not even break them up into syllables. Although he would often muddle up the order of the sounds in words, he knew a lot of words, and he could remember stories well. On the other hand he remembered songs or rhymes badly, and he had a poor sense of rhythm. All in all it seemed that his main difficulty was with organization in general and with sounds in particular, and for this reason we decided to concentrate first on organization, then on awareness of sounds, and to go on to multi-sensory methods later.

*Remediation.* Tom's written language programme began with the organization and structuring of his own language. He was encouraged, in conversation, to think carefully about what he was saying. He was set the target of writing his own book, which was to be 'published'. The book was to be typed so that he could see the words in a new setting, in typeface. One 'edition' would be the same as the original, but another would use the same words in a different context. He wanted his book to be about an airport crash truck; however we decided that 'All Sorts of Transport' would allow us more scope.

It also provided us with our first word group – 'or', the common sound in 'sorts' and 'transport'.

In four lessons, using the plastic letters, he mastered all the sound/symbol associations which he had failed to learn with the help of letter cards at school. Rules were introduced as they arose. The first one was that each syllable must contain at least one vowel. Tom had to be helped to slow down and to structure the first sentence. It began 'The airport crash truck . . . .'.

Tom was encouraged to say the word, to listen, and to say what he thought its first sound was. If he was correct, he said the whole word (or syllable) again, and then the first part of it (for example, 'crash – c', 'crash – cr'-) and listened to the word in order to hear what letter or letters he needed next.

When Tom had made the word with the letters, it was jumbled up and he had to make it again, saying and listening to each part of the word in the same way as before, as he found each letter. Tom had great difficulty with the blended sounds. But as long as the words were his and were in his vocabulary and meaningful to him he did make progress.

We began using the method of 'Simultaneous Oral Spelling' to record words he could not work out when he began to write sentences. When he made his first sentence with the letters, he recorded it in his book. He began the sentence with a capital letter and used cursive writing. He named each word before he wrote it and spelled it out at the same time. (He also illustrated his work.)

Each day Tom spent a few minutes using his plastic letters to make new words, and to generalize from these words to other words. He wrote them in his practice book using the appropriate multi-sensory method.

*Tom's progress.* He learned to recognize words more quickly than to recall them. He learned to use context and prediction in his reading so that by the time he was eight years one month his reading age (on the Neale Analysis of Reading Accuracy) was seven years, ten months, and his Comprehension eight years, one month, but on the Schonell Graded Word Reading it was only six years, six months. The Schonell Spelling age was seven years. We hear about Tom from time to time and he has been making good progress at school for several years now.

### James

*The problem.* Our next case was a boy whose problems did not fit in at all well with the major themes of this book, but who none the less did apparently flourish with the help of one of the methods that we have been advocating.

We saw him first when he was 7½ years old. He was a boy of average intelligence (IQ 98) but though he had been at school for two and a half years he had not begun to grasp even the rudiments of reading and writing, and this despite some intensive coaching. Some early sessions with him confirmed this almost total blank. He did not understand the need for a spatial separation between different written words, and when he wrote his own names (his one accomplishment in written language) he left no space between them. On the other hand his knowledge about sounds in words was quite adequate. He had been taught basic phonics and knew about letter–sound relationships. He could also judge correctly whether words rhymed or not. To that extent he was not much different from the typical six-year-old.

*James could not make the connection between spoken and written words.*

He recognized a few written words, but when he tried to read other words he used his knowledge of letter–sound relationships. He sounded out each letter (in much the same way as the child described by Prior and McCorriston – see p.114), but often got in a muddle about finding the right sounds and or about putting them together. The basic problem seemed to be that he could not make the connection between print and meaningful words. He knew that letters indicated sounds, but he had never properly understood how written words signify spoken words, probably because he did not seem to have much idea about words as separate units. Another problem was that he often confused letters which are visually similar, like 'n' and 'r'.

*Remediation.* He was seen roughly once a week over a period of a year, and each session took much the same form. He wrote a book, and had to construct each sentence in it in plastic letters first, before writing it down. James was also given the task of writing one sentence a day – with the help of his mother – about the events of the last 24 hours. He set about doing this in the same way, first setting out the sentence with plastic letters and then writing it in his diary.

It seemed that one of the advantages of handling the letters was that they helped him to see the differences between similar letters like 'n' and 'r'. The 'Simultaneous Oral Spelling' method was used to teach him not just about how to spell words, but also about written words and the significance of spaces between them.

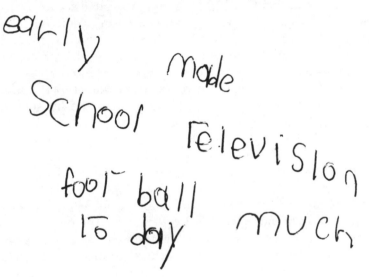

*When James was tested on the words he used in his diary he did very well.*

A little over two years after we first began to see James he was given various standardized tests again. His IQ came out rather higher (it was now 108), and his reading had caught up so that he read very nearly at the level of a typical child of his age. He was holding his own in his class at school and seemed a happy and well-adjusted child.

*Mark*

This was the boy with whom we started our book. You will remember that he often could not think of the right word and that he also had great difficulties with sounds in words. On the other hand he was able to remember words visually. For these reasons we decided to begin teaching him with words that he was most likely to know well and to be able to think of reasonably quickly. He was passionately interested in motor racing so we got him to write about that. Using the plastic letters and some new rules, such as 'tap out the syllables in the word' and 'each syllable must contain at least one vowel' he quickly worked out the sentence 'Racing car engines are normally V12.' He spontaneously discovered that 'normally' had a spelling sequence in common with 'formula'. The concentration on words that he was likely to know and the plastic letter technique which helped him over his difficulty with sounds evidently had a profound effect. He made great and continued progress. After three months his reading age had improved by 19 months and his spelling age by 17 months.

Summary

We cannot draw any firm conclusions from what has been said in this chapter. The hard evidence for the two methods that we are advocating is to be found in earlier chapters. We have simply tried to illustrate with examples of particular children what these methods actually involve. The examples themselves are not evidence and on their own do not make our case a stronger one.

If we have a new point to make it is that there is no set drill. The actual mix of methods and the way that each method is applied will vary with each child. That child's particular skills and interests and problems will determine what must be done. The methods provide a framework, and the teacher and child together must fill in the details.

## Notes

1 Checking to see that the word has been written correctly is important as backward readers are often inaccurate when they copy. Experimental data on copying is given in the chapter by Lynette Bradley in *Neuropsychology of Language, Reading and Spelling* edited by Ursula Kirk (1983).

# Epilogue

We have tried to do several things in this book. One was to explain the problems of children who fall behind in reading and the other was to find a solution to these problems. Of course we could not do either of these things completely. But the subject has taken great strides towards both goals recently, and we have done our best to show what these are. There seem to us to be two main reasons for the impressive progress in understanding and improving the plight of the backward reader. One is the co-operation between two kinds of people – people whose main concern is with theories about learning to read and people who are involved in teaching backward readers. This kind of co-operation is on the increase and it seems to us to be extraordinarily valuable. It lends reality to the theories and rigour to ideas about teaching.

The other important influence has been a growing concern with the nature of the available evidence about these children. So much of it in the past has been plainly inadequate, and the result has been a plethora of false trails. We now have a clearer idea about how to gather the right kind of information, and the result is a very much simpler picture.

That picture shows us several things. One is that the most obvious and the most consistent of the difficulties which backward readers encounter is with sounds in words. They find it hard to isolate these sounds, to use them to build words, and to see that different words have sounds in common. This means that they are slow to learn about the relationship between letters and sounds, and between groups of letters ('chunks') and sounds. The result is dire. Any child who cannot grasp these relationships is bound to fall behind in learning to read, and even further behind in learning to spell.

We also found that sensitivity to the sounds in words plays an important part in most children's success or failure in reading. It is not just a factor in the difficulties of backward readers. Backward readers are simply at the wrong end of a continuum, which stretches right through to children who do very well and much better than expected. Any child's skill with sounds will play a significant part in deciding whether he reads better or worse than would be expected, and how much better or worse. One of the important consequences of a continuum like this is the doubt that it raises about backward readers being an idiosyncratic group. Another is that it makes the idea of preventing reading problems happening a much more plausible one. There should no longer be any worries about trying to pick out the children who risk becoming backward readers, which is an impossible task anyway. If the same forces operate right through the continuum then the same experiences should help all children and not just the potential backward reader.

One kind of experience which must help, and which very young children enjoy anyway, involves playing with words and sounds. We believe that this may pave the way for the skill with sounds which has such a powerful and widespread effect when the child goes to school and begins to learn to read. Nursery rhymes and word-games are a common place in the life of the 'pre-school' child. They may play a part in children's growing sensitivity to sounds, and if they do they should become an important part in any attempt to prevent reading difficulties.

It would be foolish to claim that this was the only significant skill in learning to read or even that it was the only source of difficulty for the backward reader. Reading is a complex business which involves sophisticated intellectual moves. Logical inferences and meaningful contexts play their part too. But so far there seems to be no good reason for thinking that these cause the backward reader any particular difficulty. Certainly we should think about harnessing the backward reader's awareness of context and his interest in meaning. But we do not have to worry about teaching him these skills. There is, however, one rather sophisticated skill which seems to cause backward readers some difficulty. Making a connection between reading and spelling, and using the same strategies for the two, is an essential part of learning to read. Yet these connections do not come easily to backward readers or poor spellers. Very often they will make mistakes not through the lack of a particular strategy, but because they do not use it at the right time. They are too specialized: they tend to use one strategy in reading and not in spelling, and vice versa.

Other candidates for particular sources of difficulty for backward readers have not fared so well. The most impressive evidence for other types of difficulty comes from studies of differences among backward readers. However differences *per se* are not surprising: children do differ. No one has shown yet that backward readers fall into types which are not also to be found among other children. That crucial first step must be taken before we can use differences among backward readers as evidence for some other source of reading difficulty than the problem with sounds which we have already mentioned.

That problem seems to be well catered for by the two teaching methods which we recommend. There is good empirical evidence that these methods do work, and their success can be explained by our theory about the nature of children's reading difficulties. The first of the two methods teaches the child to put words into categories on the basis of their common sounds, and to relate these categories to particular spelling sequences. It gets the backward reader over the pernicious obstacle of his insensitivity to sounds. The second method makes connections. It shows the poor reader how the different strategies which he uses when he reads and when he spells are linked and often inter-changeable. We do not claim that these are the only ways to help the backward reader, but we have demonstrated that there are good theoretical reasons why they should work well, and we have shown that they do.

Psychologists and teachers have done well in their search for ways of helping the child who is in difficulty with reading. So long as they keep on working together, they can be sure of more and more success.

# References

Baddeley, A.D., Ellis, N.C., Miles, T.R. and Lewis, V.J. (1982) 'Developmental and Acquired Dyslexia: a Comparison', *Cognition, 11,* 185–99.

Bakker, D.J. (1967) 'Temporal Order, Meaningfulness and Reading Ability', *Perceptual and Motor Skills, 24,* 1027–30.

Barron, R.W. (1980) 'Visual–Orthographic and Phonological Strategies in Reading and Spelling', U. Frith (ed.), *Cognitive Processes in Spelling* (London: Academic Press).

Barron, R. and Baron, J. (1977) 'How Children Get Meaning from Printed Words', *Child Development, 48,* 587–94.

Bertelson, P., Morais, J., Alegria, J. and Content, A. (1985) 'Phonetic Analysis Capacity', *Nature* (in press).

Birch, H. and Belmont, A. (1964) 'Auditory-Visual Integration in Normal and Retarded Readers', *American Journal of Orthopsychiatry, 34,* 852–61.

Bishop, D.V.M. and Butterworth, G.E. (1980) 'Verbal-Performance Discrepancies: Relationship to Birth Risk and Specific Reading Retardation', *Cortex, 16,* 375–90.

Boder, E. (1973) 'Developmental Dyslexia: a Diagnostic Approach Based on Three Atypical Reading-spelling Patterns', *Developmental Medicine and Child Neurology, 15,* 663–87.

Bouma, H. and Legein, C.P. (1981) 'Visual Recognition Experiments in Dyslexia', in G.Th. Pavlides and T.R. Miles (eds), *Dyslexia Research and its Applications to Education* (London: John Wiley).

Bradley, L. (1981a) 'A Tactile Approach to Reading', *British Journal of Special Education: Forward Trends, 8,* no. 4, 32–6.

Bradley, L. (1981b) *Sound Pictures* (Basingstoke & London: Macmillan).

Bradley, L. (1981c) 'The Organisation of Motor Patterns for Spelling: an Effective Remedial Strategy for Backward Readers, *Developmental Medicine and Child Neurology, 23,* 83–91.

Bradley, L. (1983) 'The Organisation of Visual, Phonological and Motor Strategies in Learning to Read and to Spell', in U. Kirk (ed.), *Neuropsychology of Language, Reading and Spelling* (New York: Academic Press).

Bradley, L. (1984) *Assessing Reading Difficulties: A Diagnostic and Remedial Approach,* 2nd edn (London & Basingstoke: Macmillan)

Bradley, L. and Bryant, P.E. (1978) 'Difficulties in Auditory Organisation as a Possible Cause of Reading Backwardness', *Nature*, 271, 746–7.

Bradley, L. and Bryant, P.E. (1979) 'The Independence of Reading and Spelling in Backward and Normal Readers', *Developmental Medicine and Child Neurology*, 21, 504–14.

Bradley, L. and Bryant, P.E. (1983) 'Categorising Sounds and Learning to Read: a Causal Connexion', *Nature*, 301, 419–21.

Bradley, L. and Bryant, P. (1985) *Rhyme and Reason in Reading and Spelling* (Ann Arbor: University of Michigan Press).

Bradley, L., Hulme, C. and Bryant, P.E. (1979) 'The Connexion Between Different Verbal Difficulties in a Backward Reader: a Case Study', *Developmental Medicine and Child Neurology*, 21, 790–5.

Branwhite, A.B. (1983) 'Boosting Reading Skills by Direct Instruction', *British Journal of Educational Psychology*, 53, 267–77.

Bruce, D.J. (1964) 'The Analysis of Word Sounds', *British Journal of Educational Psychology*, 34, 158–70.

Bryant, P. (1974) *Perception and Understanding in Young Children* (London: Methuen).

Bryant, P.E. (1975) 'Cross-modal Development and Reading', in D.D. Duane and M.B. Rawson (eds), *Reading, Perception and Language* (Baltimore: York Press).

Bryant, P.E. (1983) 'The Next Moves', in J.P. Das, R.F. Mulcahy and A.E. Wall (eds), *Theory and Research in Learning Disabilities* (New York: Plenum Press).

Bryant, P. and Bradley, L. (1980) 'Why Children Sometimes Write Words which They Cannot Read', in U. Frith (ed.), *Cognitive Processes in Spelling* (London: Academic Press).

Bryant, P.E. and Bradley, L. (1983a) 'Psychological Strategies and the Development of Reading and Writing', in M. Martlew (ed.), *The Psychology of Written Language* (Chichester: J. Wiley).

Bryant, P.E. and Bradley, L. (1983b) 'Auditory Organisation and Backwardness in Reading', in M. Rutter (1983).

Bryant, P.E. and Bradley, L. (1985) 'Phonetic Analysis Capacity and Learning to Read', *Nature*, 313, 73–4.

Bryant, P. and Kopytynska, H. (1976) 'Spontaneous Measurement by Children', *Nature*, 260, 773.

Bryden, M.P. (1972) 'Auditory–Visual and Sequential–Spatial Matching in Relation to Reading Ability', *Child Development*, 43, 824–32.

Chukovsky, K. (1963) *From Two to Five* (Berkely and Los Angeles: University of California Press).

Coltheart, M., Masterson, J., Byng, S., Prior, M. and Riddoch, J. (1983) 'Surface Dyslexia', *Quarterly Journal of Experimental Psychology*, 35, 469–95.

Denckla, M. and Rudel, R. (1976) 'Rapid Automatised Naming: Dyslexia Differentiated from Other Learning Disabilities', *Neuropsychologia*, 14, 471–9.

Doctor, E.A. and Coltheart, M. (1980) 'Children's Use of Phonological Encoding when Reading for Meaning', *Memory and Cognition, 8,* 195–209.

Ellis, A. (1984) *Reading, Writing and Dyslexia* (London: Lawrence Erlbaum).

Fernald, G.M. (1943) *Remedial Techniques in Basic School Subjects* (New York: McGraw-Hill).

Ferreiro, E. and Teberosky, A. (1979) *Literacy before Schooling* (London: Heinemann Educational).

Fox, B. and Routh, D.K. (1976) 'Phonemic Analysis and Synthesis as Word Attack Skills', *Journal of Educational Psychology, 68,* 70–4.

Fox, B. and Routh, D.K. (1983) 'Reading Disability, Phonemic Analysis, and Dysphonetic Spelling: a follow-up Study', *Journal of Clinical Child Psychology, 12,* 28–32.

Frith, U. (1970) 'Studies in Pattern Detection in Normal and Autistic Children: Reproduction and Production of Colour Sequences', *Journal of Experimental Child Psychology, 10,* 120–35.

Frith, U. (1980) 'Unexpected Spelling Problems', in U. Frith (ed.), *Cognitive Processes in Spelling* (London: Academic Press).

Frith, U. and Snowling, M. (1983) 'Reading for Meaning and Reading for Sound in Autistic and Dyslexic Children', *British Journal of Developmental Psychology, 1,* 329–42.

Gelb, I.J. (1963) *A Study of Writing,* 2nd edn (Chicago: University of Chicago Press).

Gillingham, A.M. and Stillman, B.U. (1956) *Remedial Training for Children with Specific Disability in Reading, Spelling and Penmanship,* 5th edn (New York: Sackett & Wilhelms).

Gittelman, R. (1983) 'Treatment of Reading Disorders', in M. Rutter (ed.), *Developmental Neuropsychiatry* (New York: Guilford Press).

Gittelman, R. and Feingold, I. (1983) 'Children with Reading Disorders – I: Efficacy of Reading Remediation', *Journal of Child Psychology and Psychiatry, 24,* 167–92.

Goldstein, D.M. (1976) 'Cognitive–Linguistic Functioning and Learning to Read in Preschoolers', *Journal of Educational Psychology, 68,* 680–8.

Goodman, K. (1982) *Language and Literacy* (Boston: Routledge & Kegan Paul).

Guthrie, I.T. (1973) 'Reading Comprehension and Synctactic Responses in Good and Poor Readers', *Journal of Educational Psychology, 65,* 294–9.

Henderson, L. (1982) *Orthography and Word Recognition in Reading* (London: Academic Press).

Hewison, J. and Tizard, J. (1980) 'Parental Involvement and Reading Attainment', *British Journal of Educational Psychology, 50,* 209–15.

Hewison, J., Tizard, J. and Schofield, W.N. (1982) 'Collaboration between Teachers and Parents in Assisting Children's Reading', *British Journal of Educational Psychology, 52,* 1–15.

Hinshelwood, J. (1895) 'Word-blindness and Visual Memory', *Lancet, 2,* 1564–70.

Holmes, D.R. and McKeever, W.F. (1979) 'Material Specific Serial Memory Deficit in Adolescent Dyslexics', *Cortex, 15,* 51–62.

Holmes, V.L. and Pepper, R.J. (1977) 'An Evaluation of Spelling Error Analysis in the Diagnosis of Reading Disability', *Child Development, 48,* 1708–11.

Hornsby, B. and Miles, T. (1980) 'The Effects of a Dyslexia-centred Teaching Programme', *British Journal of Educational Psychology, 50,* 236–42.

Hulme, C. (1981) *Reading Retardation and Multi-sensory Teaching* (London: Routledge & Kegan Paul).

Jorm, A.F. (1979) 'The Cognitive and Neurological Basis of Developmental Dyslexia: a Theoretical Framework and Review', *Cognition, 7,* 19–32.

Jorm, A.F. (1983) 'Specific Reading Retardation and Working Memory: a Review', *British Journal of Psychology, 74,* 311–42.

Kimura, Y. and Bryant, P.E. (1983) 'Reading and Writing in English and Japanese', *British Journal of Developmental Psychology, 1,* 129–44.

Kress, G. (1982) *Learning to Write* (London: Routledge & Kegan Paul).

Liberman, I.Y., Mann, V.A., Shankweiler, D. and Werfelman, D. (1982) 'Children's memory for recurring linguistic and non-linguistic material in relation to reading ability', *Cortex, 18,* 367–75.

Liberman, I.Y., Shankweiler, D., Orland, C., Harris, K.S. and Berti, F.B. (1971) 'Letter Confusion and Reversals of Sequence in the Beginning Reader: Implications for Orton's Theory of Dyslexia', *Cortex, 7,* 127–42.

Liberman, I.Y., Shankweiler, D., Liberman, A.M., Fowler, C. and Fischer, F.W. (1978) 'Phonetic Segmentation and Recoding in the Beginning Reader', in A.S. Reber and D.L. Scarborough (eds), *Toward a Psychology of Reading* (New York: Lawrence Erlbaum).

Lundberg, I., Olofsson, A. and Wall, S. (1981) 'Reading and Spelling Skills in the First School Years Predicted from Phonemic Awareness Skills in Kindergarten', *Scandanavian Journal of Psychology, 21,* 159–73.

Lyle, J. (1969) 'Reading Retardation and Reversal Tendency: a Factorial Study', *Child Development, 41,* 481–91.

Lyle, J. and Goyen, J. (1975) 'Effect of Speed of Exposure and Difficulty of Discrimination on Visual Recognition of Retarded Readers', *Journal of Abnormal Psychology, 84,* 673–6.

McGarrigle, J. and Donaldson, M. (1974) 'Conservation Accidents', *Cognition, 3,* 341–50.

Marcel, T. (1980) 'Phonological Awareness and Phonological Representation: Investingation of a Specific Spelling Problem', in U. Frith (ed.), *Cognitive Processes in Spelling* (London: Academic Press).

Marsh, G. and Desberg, P. (1983) 'The Development of Strategies in the Acquisition of Symbolic Skills', in D.R. Rogers and J. Sloboda (eds), *The Acquisition of Symbolic Skills* (NATO Conference Series III:2. New York: Plenum Press).

Marshall, J. and Newcombe, F. (1966) 'Syntactic and Semantic Errors in

Paralexia', *Neuropsychologia, 4,* 169–76.

Mitterer, J.O. (1982) 'There are at least Two Kinds of Poor Readers: Whole Word Poor Readers and Recoding Poor Readers', *Canadian Journal of Psychology, 36,* 445–61.

Montessori, M. (1915) *The Montessori Method* (London: Heinemann).

Morais, J., Cary, L., Alegria, J. and Bertelson, P. (1979) 'Does Awareness of Speech as a Sequence of Phones Arise Spontaneously?', *Cognition, 7,* 323–3.

Morgan, W. Pringle (1896) 'A Case of Congenital Word Blindness', *British Medical Journal, 2,* 1378.

Naidoo, S. (1981) 'Teaching Methods and their Rationale', in G. Th. Pavlidis and T.R. Miles (eds), *Dyslexia Research and its Application to Education* (London: John Wiley).

Olofsson, A. and Lundberg, I. (1983) 'Can Phonemic Awareness be Trained in Kindergarten?', *Scandinavian Journal of Psychology, 24,* 35–44.

Orton, S.T. (1928) 'Specific Reading Disability–Strephosymbolia', *Journal of the American Medical Association, 90,* 1095–9.

Perfetti, C.A and Hogaboam, T. (1975) 'Relationship between Single Word Decoding and Reading Comprehension Skill', *Journal of Educational Psychology, 67,* 461–9.

Perfetti, C., Goldman, S. and Hogaboam, T. (1979) 'Reading Skill and the Identification of Words in Discourse Context', *Memory and Cognition, 7,* 273–82.

Piaget, J. (1972) *The Principles of Genetic Epistemology* (London: Routledge & Kegan Paul).

Piaget, J. (1978) *The Grasp of Consciousness* (London: Routledge & Kegan Paul).

Piaget, J. Inhelder, B. and Szeminska, A. (1960) *The Child's Conception of Geometry* (London: Routledge & Kegan Paul).

Piaget, J. and Szeminska, A. (1952) *The Child's Conception of Number* (London: Routledge & Kegan Paul).

Prior, M. and McCorriston, M. (1983) 'Acquired and Developmental Spelling Dyslexia', *Brain and Language, 20,* 263–85.

Read, C. (1971) 'Pre-school Children's Knowledge of English Phonology', *Harvard Educational Review, 41,* 1–34.

Read, C. (1978) 'Children's Awareness of Language, with Emphasis on Sound Systems', in A. Sinclair, R.J. Jarvella and W.J.M. Levelt (eds), *The Child's Conception of Language* (Berlin: Springer).

Robertson, S. (1984) 'Children's Strategies in the Development of Reading and Spelling', unpublished D.Phil. thesis, Oxford.

Rodgers, B. (1983) 'The Identification and Prevalence of Specific Reading Retardation', *British Journal of Educational Psychology, 53,* 369–73.

Rutter, M. (ed.) (1983) *Developmental Neuropsychiatry* (New York: Guilford Press).

Rutter, M. and Yule, W. (1975) 'The Concept of Specific Reading

Retardation', *Journal of Child Psychology and Psychiatry, 16,* 181–97.

Slobin, D.I. (1978) *Studies of Child Language Development* (New York: Holt, Rinehart & Winston).

Smith, F. (1978) *Understanding Reading,* 2nd edn (New York: Holt, Rinehart & Winston).

Snowling, M.J. (1980) 'The Development of Grapheme–phoneme Correspondence in Normal and Dyslexic Readers, *Journal of Experimental Child Psychology, 29,* 294–305.

Standing, E.M. (1957) *Maria Montessori: Her Life and Work* (New York: Hollis & Carter).

Stevenson, H.W., Stigler, J.W., Lucker, G.W., Lee, S.-Y., Hsu, C.-C. and Kitamura, S. (1982) 'Reading Disabilities: the Case of Chinese, Japanese and English', *Child Development, 53,* 1164–81.

Temple, C. and Marshall, J. (1983) 'A Case Study of Developmental Phonological Dyslexia', *British Journal of Psychology, 74,* 517–33.

Treiman, R. and Baron, J. (1981) 'Segmental analysis ability: Development and relation to reading ability', in G.C. MacKinnon and T.G. Waller (eds), *Reading Research: Advances in Theory and Practice. (Vol III)* (New York: Academic Press).

Vellutino, F.R. (1979) *Dyslexia* (Cambridge, Mass.: MIT Press).

Williams, J. (1980) 'Teaching Decoding with an Emphasis on Phoneme Analysis and Phoneme Blending', *Journal of Educational Psychology, 72,* 1–15.

Yule, W., Rutter, M., Berger, M. and Thompson, J. (1974) 'Over and Under Achievement in Reading: Distribution in the General Population', *British Journal of Educational Psychology, 44,* 1–11.

# Index